REMEMBERING

MILLEDGEVILLE

REMEMBERING

MILLEDGEVILLE

HISTORIC TALES FROM
Georgia's Antebellum Capital

HUGH T. HARRINGTON

THE
History
PRESS

Published by The History Press
Charleston, SC 29403
www.historypress.net

Cover design by Natasha Momberger.

Front cover: Old Governor's Mansion. *Courtesy of the Library of Congress.*
Back cover: Old State Capitol, Gates from the South. *Courtesy of the Library of Congress.*

First published 2005
Second printing 2008

978-1-5402-0371-7

Library of Congress Cataloging-in-Publication Data

Harrington, Hugh T. (Hugh Thompson)
Remembering Milledgeville : historic tales from Georgia's antebellum
capital / Hugh T. Harrington.
p. cm.
Includes index.
ISBN 1-59629-041-2 (alk. paper)
1. Milledgeville (Ga.)--History--Anecdotes. I. Title.
F294.M6H37 2005
975.8'573--dc22
2005008816

To:

My grandmother, Caroline Thompson Harrington (1874–1969),
who first encouraged me to study history.

My grandfather, William Harold "Hal" Whiteley (1890–1978), the publisher and editor of
The Presque Isle County Advance, *who showed me how to write.*

My father, William Henry Harrington (1912–1994),
who taught me the importance of a "feel for history."

CONTENTS

Acknowledgements	9
Preface	11
Dr. John Ruggles Cotting: More Than Just a "Former State of Georgia Geologist"	13
Buffalo Soldiers in Memory Hill Cemetery	15
The Strange Imprisonment of Thomas Fair	17
Tomlinson Fort and Milledgeville's Smallpox Epidemic of 1835	19
Wilkinson—A Street Named for a Scoundrel	21
The Convicted Murderer and the Georgia Legislature	23
The Sculpture by Robert E. Launitz	25
Ty Cobb in Milledgeville	27
The Great Earthquake of 1886	29
President McKinley's Visit to Milledgeville	31
The History of Parson Weems	33
A Tornado Almost Destroys Milledgeville in 1875	35
Abner Hammond—The Man with Two Graves	37
"The Stars Are Falling!"—The Great Meteor Shower of 1833	39
Abner Hammond's Fight with Governor John Clark	41
Chatham Street	43
Thomas Petters Carnes—Revolutionary War Soldier	45
Georgia Normal and Industrial College's Forgotten Tragedy	47
Two Memory Hill Mysteries	49
Cannons Can Be Dangerous	51
"I Have Seen the Giraffe!"	53
Lincoln Street	55
Montgomery Street	57
Stories Behind the Zinc Tombstone of John Sherrod Thomas	59
Medieval Knights Vie for Love and Beauty in Milledgeville	61
The Old Capitol Base Ball Club of 1871	63
Milledgeville's First Velocipede	65
Milledgeville's First Museum	67
Cause of Death: Teething!	69
The Spectacular Sunsets of 1883	71
Animals on the Streets	73
Echoes of Lafayette's Visit to Milledgeville	75
Jett Thomas's Unique Dying Proposition	77
Mad Dog!	79
The Dramatic End to the Life of Henry Byrom, Gambler	81
Old Jim	83

The Presidential Candidate from Milledgeville   85
Hillsborough—Baldwin County's First Courthouse   87
The Great Rooster Rip-Off of 1903   89
The Ladies' Artillery Company of Jefferson Street   91
Joanna Troutman and the Flag of Texas   93
The Battle of the Baldwin-Putnam Bridge   95
Benjamin Talbert—Revolutionary Soldier   97
Dr. B.J. Simmons   99
The Murder of Lemuel Smith   101
The Murder of Lewis H. Kenan   103
General Anthony Wayne Reminds Us That History Is Not Boring   105
General Nathanael Greene's Hat   107
Flying over Milledgeville, 1877 Style   109
The Gwinnett-McIntosh Duel   111
The Voodoo Murders   113
Get Your Head Examined   115
Old Milledgeville Lamar Myth Replaced with Fact   117
A Cure for the Common Scold   121
Milledgeville Reading Room   123
Salubrious Milledgeville...Or Is It?   125
The Killing of Deputy Marshal Charles Haygood   127
Dixie Haygood and the Magic of Her Annie Abbott Act   129
The Expulsion of Henry E. Kreutz   131
Major General Joseph Warren's Teeth   133
A Case of Bigamy   135
The Mysterious Duel of James Spalding   137
The Harris-Sanford Murder   139
The State House Fire of 1833   141
Husband Illegally Puts His Wife in Asylum   143
Treating a Scalped Head   145
Never Pull an Arrow Out of a Body   147
George Washington's First Crisis as Commanding General   149

Index   155

ACKNOWLEDGEMENTS

I DID NOT WRITE THIS BOOK alone—I could not have done so. I needed many people to pass interesting stories in my direction. Others would supply sources of information when I was at a loss for materials. Many went out of their way to give me encouragement. Far more people have helped me in this project than I am able to thank individually. If it had not been for the accumulated assistance I received from so many, the glimpses into our past provided in this book would never have occurred.

I particularly want to thank Nancy Davis Bray, the university archivist of Georgia College & State University, and Tammy Wyatt, archival associate for unfailingly, and cheerfully, locating sources and images whenever asked. Mary Moore Jones, head of interlibrary loan, always came through when I was seeking some obscure item. Eileen Babb McAdams has been singularly helpful with her enthusiastic support, suggestions of topics and generously sharing her own research with me on many occasions. Robert S. Davis shared a breakthrough with me regarding the 1832 Johnson murder.

Anne Buckner Burgamy frequently provided much needed advice and suggestions. Others who have helped in a multitude of ways are Louise Horne, Anne King, Betty Dawson and Floride Gardner. Pam Beer, editor of the *Baldwin Bulletin*, graciously allowed me to write my column, "'Round and About."

Last, but most importantly, I want to thank my wife Sue. Despite her excellent education and vast experience, she does not know the meaning of the word "impossible." Without her constant help and support, this project, and so many others, would never have gotten off the ground.

PREFACE

THE PAST OF MILLEDGEVILLE, BALDWIN County and central Georgia is slipping away. What was considered common knowledge 100 or 150 years ago is now becoming obscured or entirely forgotten. Legends, myths and complete ignorance are fast replacing known facts about the past.

I have consciously sought to bring to light some of the less well known, or unknown, people and events from the nineteenth century. I would like to think that stories connected with central Georgia history may appeal to people who are interested in history wherever they may reside. Much of what I write about was important at the time but now is often unknown entirely. I am not a professional historian and certainly not the best qualified person for this task. However, as the preservation of these glimpses of our history is a task that no one else has undertaken, I believe it is better to have it from my pen than not have it at all.

Readers of the *Baldwin Bulletin* will recognize many of these chapters as having appeared, often in a somewhat different form, in my "'Round and About" column. These faithful readers first suggested compiling my columns into book form to make them more accessible.

My principle sources are the old newspapers of Milledgeville. The *Georgia Journal, Southern Recorder, Federal Union, Union-Recorder* and others less well known provide a wealth of information. The only effective way to search them is to read them. Indexes and abstracts, while very helpful, only cover a small percentage of the information in the papers. These newspapers are available at the Georgia College & State University library and Mary Vinson Memorial Library on microfilm. I also sought out the views from other newspapers not domiciled in Milledgeville. A surprising number of interesting articles on events in and around Milledgeville appeared elsewhere while the local papers ignored them. The *New York Times* and the *Atlanta Journal-Constitution* seemed to cover many central Georgia events. Wherever possible I sought out primary sources in an effort to avoid the myths and legends secondary sources often perpetuate.

I have written these historical stories for the general reader. It is my hope that these short accounts will be entertaining as well as enlightening. I would be pleased if they spark interest in some readers to do further research. While I have done my best to be as accurate as possible, I am sure that only rarely do I have the whole story. There is much left to uncover, rediscover and enjoy.

Hugh T. Harrington
Milledgeville, Georgia

DR. JOHN RUGGLES COTTING: MORE THAN JUST A "FORMER STATE OF GEORGIA GEOLOGIST"

T HE OTHER DAY I WAS walking through Milledgeville's best kept secret: Memory Hill Cemetery. I've passed by the gravestone and the bronze plaque of "Dr. John Ruggles Cotting, 1784–1867, Former State of Georgia Geologist" many times. I never paid much attention to it. The man was a geologist. That just doesn't sound very interesting to me. As is often the case, I was wrong.

After a bit of research, I find that Dr. Cotting was indeed more than a geologist. He was very well educated in science, made numerous contributions to scientific literature and was an educator, a minister and a humble, peaceful and scholarly gentleman.

Cotting was a Yankee, in the traditional sense, being born in Acton, Massachusetts, in 1784. He attended Harvard College, withdrawing twice due to poor health. He graduated from Dartmouth College in 1802. He was a professor at Amherst College, the Berkshire Medical Institute (Williams College) and several other schools in New England where he taught chemistry, botany, experimental philosophy and geology. He also taught in and ran his own schools.

In 1822, he published a college textbook called *An Introduction to Chemistry*, which he followed in 1825 with *Lectures on Geology*. In 1826, he was editor and publisher of *The Chemist and Meteorological Journal*.

In 1810, he was ordained as a Congregational minister but continued his work with science. He left the church in 1812 and became an Episcopalian. Later, in Milledgeville, he was active in establishing St. Stephen's Episcopal Church where he served for over twenty years as a vestryman.

His obituary says that he had no heart "for the material, transitory interests" that engage most men. Rather, he "loved the serene realms of philosophy, where the pursuit of knowledge is endless and the purest pleasures are obtained without rivalry or strife." He was a "purified, exalted, refined spirit, an alien to the busy throng of material men."

He did not deal entirely in philosophical work, however. In the War of 1812, he, along with other "chemists and capitalists in Boston," engaged in "manufacturing several articles never before produced in America." I have no idea just what that means. I presume his work had something to do with explosives or incendiary devices. I would be interested to know more about this work.

In 1835, he left Massachusetts and moved to Augusta, Georgia. He was retained by citizens of Burke and Richmond Counties to survey the soils and geology of the counties. He expanded on his work with soil and collected three hundred species of fossils and one thousand plants. His report on this project reached 198 pages.

Georgia legislators took notice of his work and authorized a statewide survey of the geology of Georgia. Cotting was appointed the state geologist in 1836 and moved to Milledgeville to begin the massive survey. His work was never completed nor published. The state abolished his office in 1840. Cotting, however, continued to refer to himself as the state geologist.

In 1843, Cotting published "An Essay on the Soils and Available Manures of the State of Georgia, with the Mode of Application and Management, Founded on a Geological and Agricultural Survey." Interestingly, he commented in this essay that "the worn out fields, the gullied hills and barren wastes in every part of the State . . . are sad mementoes of the effect of ignorance and prejudice on the part of our predecessors." Clearly, Cotting was ahead of his time in the field of agriculture.

In the 1840s, Cotting, aided by his wife, established an academy in Milledgeville. I have not yet located where it was housed but presume that the building is no longer standing. He wrote articles for *The Southern Medical and Surgical Journal*, including one on clay eating.

Cotting's obituary says that "his thirty years of life at Milledgeville were unblemished years of innocence, goodness and activity. His maxim was, 'Wear out, not rust out.' Eminent among us for a heart and life without guile and a hand ever busy, even to old age, with duty, he lived beloved, and has died in honor, as the righteous die, a death of peace." How nice it would be to have such words said about me in my obituary, but, as I am sure my wife agrees, the sentiment doesn't fit me.

Now, when standing at the gravesite of Dr. Cotting, I see more than just "former State of Georgia Geologist." I see a man of science, religion and education whose story I have glimpsed. Looking around at the peaceful and beautiful cemetery, there are hundreds of graves within sight. All of these people have their own stories to tell. And what fascinating stories they are.

BUFFALO SOLDIERS IN MEMORY HILL CEMETERY

IN THE QUIET SHADE OF the old trees in Memory Hill Cemetery rest veterans from many wars. These men and women served in all branches of the armed services in conflicts from the Revolutionary War to modern times. Some are prominent and some are honored yearly, while others are less well remembered. I don't refer to these veterans as forgotten because not only have I not forgotten them, but we as a people cannot allow ourselves to forget them.

Three of the less well remembered are Buffalo Soldiers. In 1866, the Ninth and Tenth U.S. Cavalry Regiments and the Twenty-fourth and Twenty-fifth Infantry Regiments were formed. The officers were white and the enlisted men were black. The Buffalo Soldiers are best known for their service in the West fighting Indians. Some people may recall the 1960 movie *Sergeant Rutledge* or the 1997 movie *The Buffalo Soldiers*. The Buffalo Soldiers did more than patrol the West and fight Indians. In 1898, they were sent to Cuba to participate in the Spanish-American War. A year later, they were sent to the Philippines to fight in the Philippine-American War. They fought in World War I and also against Pancho Villa along the U.S. border with Mexico.

Everyone has heard of Teddy Roosevelt and his "Rough Riders" and their charge up San Juan Hill in Cuba during the Spanish-American War. It often appears as if he and his men were alone. However, that was hardly the case. The "Rough Riders" were just one of the fifteen regiments consisting of over eight thousand Americans involved in that attack. The Ninth and Tenth Cavalry and the Twenty-fourth Infantry regiments were there and also fought their way up San Juan Hill alongside the white regiments, including the Rough Riders. The cavalry did not have horses, so they fought on foot as dismounted cavalry.

The three Buffalo Soldiers in Memory Hill are Robert Lee (1878–1924), James A. Gibson (1880–1945) and Sol Sanford (1878–1925), all in the Ninth Cavalry. In the 1900 census, the three are listed as belonging to Troop H, Ninth U.S. Cavalry stationed at Fort Wingate, New Mexico. In addition, two more Milledgeville men, George Clark and Emmett Brooks, are listed. The burial locations of Clark and Brooks are unknown. Another soldier, Private George W. Scott, who was born in March 1879 in Milledgeville, was at Fort Huachuca,

Arizona, for the 1900 census. In 1910, Private George W. Scott was at Fort D.A. Russell in Wyoming. He was married but his wife's name was not listed.

Sol Sanford, and probably the others as well, participated in the Spanish-American War. They almost certainly were involved in the July 1, 1898 attack on San Juan Hill along with Teddy Roosevelt and his Rough Riders. Sanford also was awarded a sharpshooter's medal. In 1900, he and Troop H were sent to the Philippine-American War.

The 1910 census places Sol Sanford at Fort D.A. Russell in Laramie County, Wyoming. He was a wagoner and still in Troop H, Ninth Cavalry.

The black Americans who fought in Cuba were at the time hailed as heroes for their exploits. Now, the events they participated in and the men themselves are less well remembered. Perhaps for the first time, we have a glimpse of the local men who became Buffalo Soldiers and an idea of what they did.

I hope that people in Milledgeville take a look back into their collective past for bits and pieces of information that may lead to a more complete picture of Sol Sanford, Robert Lee and James A. Gibson as well as George Clark and Emmett Brooks. We cannot allow these men to fall into the category of "forgotten."

The Strange Imprisonment
of Thomas Fair

Old newspapers sometimes publish an odd article that is entirely unexpected and has a peculiar story behind it. This is the situation with the obituary of Thomas Fair of Milledgeville.

Thomas Fair was born around 1825. He was the eldest son of Colonel Peter Fair and the grandson of Revolutionary War veteran Peter Fair. He volunteered for the Confederate army in June of 1861 and became a private in Company F, Ninth Georgia Infantry. He soon was made a corporal and later a sergeant. He served throughout the war and surrendered at Appomattox, Virginia, on April 9, 1865. His was the career of an honorable soldier.

When he died January 28, 1894, of "paralysis of the brain," the newspaper carried an obituary that said in part:

The death of Mr. Tom Fair, which occurred at the home of his brothers in this city, about 8 o'clock last Sunday night was heard with surprise by our citizens. His presence in the city was known to only a few persons. He...spent his life in this city up to 1874, when he left here, except for the four years he spent in the army.

He had left the city in 1874 and then died. Nothing very strange about that. But there is more to the story. His death was a "surprise." The newspaper was being especially discreet as there were circumstances that make Thomas Fair's life very unusual.

Tom Fair left Milledgeville the evening of August 15, 1874, in a hurry. He had just killed a man and was on the run. Apparently, while intoxicated, he had been visiting a house of ill repute and engaged in a fight with a man named Oliver Ellison. In the course of the fight, Fair stabbed Ellison with a knife. A few hours later, twenty-two-year-old Oliver Ellison was dead and forty-nine-year-old Tom Fair was on the run.

Tom Fair was indicted for murder. The relatives of Oliver Ellison searched the country for Fair but he could not be located. He had disappeared completely. Twenty years later, he reappeared, dead, in Milledgeville. That was the "surprise" mentioned in the obituary.

Where had he been for those twenty years? His whereabouts for the first seven years are unknown but it is thought that he went to Louisiana, Texas and the far West. However, for his last thirteen years he was in Milledgeville. He returned one night and stayed with his family, never venturing outside during daylight. Only the immediate family knew he had returned and they kept his secret for thirteen years. All that time he was imprisoned within a family member's house in downtown Milledgeville.

Today his grave in Memory Hill is marked with a Confederate veteran's marble marker in the same lot with his father and famous grandfather. And, Oliver Ellison, the man he killed, lies in a grave less than thirty yards away. It is thought that Thomas Fair would leave the sanctuary of the house at night and walk the streets of Milledgeville in the dark. One wonders if he ever visited Ellison's grave and what his thoughts might have been as he contemplated the event that ruined two lives.

Tomlinson Fort and Milledgeville's Smallpox Epidemic of 1835

Smallpox! Today the very word sends shivers down the spine. In 1835 the reaction to the mention of smallpox was far more severe. This highly contagious disease was greatly feared in Milledgeville. Dr. Edward Jenner's smallpox vaccination had long been available but was not widely accepted. Many who were immune had not been vaccinated but rather had contracted smallpox and survived.

In January of 1835, Milledgeville newspapers carried a notice that Dr. Tomlinson Fort had "fresh vaccine matter" that he would distribute to other physicians. This material had been "procured by his Excellency the Governor" by a resolution of the state legislature to provide free vaccinations for everyone. The governor at that time was William Lumpkin.

In late April, another announcement appeared. This time it was ominous. Under the heading "Small Pox," the notice stated that "The physicians of Milledgeville announce to the community that this disease has made its appearance amongst us." They went on to say that there was only one case and it had existed for ten days "and bids fair to terminate favorably" and that there is "no evidence that it will spread further and a vigorous effort to secure the benefits of vaccination is in operation." In other words, the disease is here, let's not panic but get vaccinated fast.

A few days later another short announcement appeared saying, with a sigh of relief, that it is "our pleasant duty to announce that no new case of the small pox has occurred in Milledgeville; and we believe after strict inquiry, that there are no symptoms of any new case."

Then, May 5, 1835, notices again appeared in the Milledgeville papers. They announced the death, by smallpox, of John W.R. Clark, son of former Governor John Clark. However, in the same notices, both papers also tried to alleviate the fears of the population. The *Federal Union* started their notice not by mentioning the death but by saying, "No new case of this disease has occurred, nor have any symptoms of a recurrence shown themselves. The first and last case in Milledgeville terminated fatally." The short notice ended by saying, "Every sanitary measure, that prudence suggested, has, we understand, been adopted, to extirpate the contagion. In visiting our town, no danger need, we think, be apprehended."

The *Southern Recorder* did not name Clark as the victim, only saying that "the case of Small Pox hitherto reported, terminated fatally." The paper then went on to say no other case had occurred. Interestingly, the paper mentions that "our town has for a week or two past presented but a dull appearance, in comparison with its usual air of life and business."

The May 12 *Southern Recorder* tells us that "a little alarm and excitement was produced on Sunday last, from another supposed case of Small Pox." The patient, a Mr. Breedlove, was put in the hospital building set aside for smallpox patients and a guard was placed on the premises to ensure that no one came in contact with the patient due to the fear of spreading the disease. At first the physicians thought, and hoped, that the patient really didn't have smallpox but rather was suffering from the effects of inoculation. Nevertheless, they soon realized that this was actually a smallpox case.

Surprisingly, and unheard of in today's world, the May 12 *Southern Recorder* carried an open letter from twenty-six prominent men of Milledgeville addressed to Dr. Tomlinson Fort. The letter expressed their unqualified approval of Fort's conduct in giving care to the patient John Clark: "you fearlessly did whatever professional duty required of you." They further stated that if Fort "should be doomed to be a sufferer, yet in the midst of the affliction you will have the same proud and ennobling consolation to sustain you, under the trial. Of one thing, be assured, whatever may betide you, you have our sincere wishes for your future health and happiness."

Tomlinson Fort's reply was also printed. It's a remarkable letter so I'm going to quote a lot of it. He said the letter from the citizens was "received, and perused with peculiar emotion." Fort said he

regarded the duty of facing pestilential diseases as sacred as it is awful. The great body of my profession have for ages practiced on this moral, and thousands have perished in its support. I rejoice that you think I have not tarnished the luster of these dear bought honors. A short time will prove whether I have passed safely through a great exposure to a horrible contagion. I am shielded by the immortal discovery of Jenner; but sad is the reflection, that the benefits of this discovery, although very great are less to be relied on than formerly. But should I experience, in my own person, the insufficiency of vaccination, and thus become the cause of a destroying pestilence in my own family; nay, should death itself number me with those who have fallen in this great cause, the sentiments expressed by you, gentlemen, will buoy me up, and I humbly trust, I shall feel not a sentiment of regret or remorse, that I have been thus called to the last scene of a laborious life.

Fort did not get smallpox.

But, there is more to the story of John Clark and Tomlinson Fort. As was customary, Clark was put in the pesthouse on the outskirts of town. A mass meeting in Milledgeville demanded that Fort stop treating Clark for fear Fort might spread the disease. The door to Clark's room was padlocked. Tomlinson Fort climbed a ladder to get into the sickroom through a window. He continued to treat Clark, with a gun at his side, until Clark died. After going through this ordeal, he must have felt, as Fort said, a "peculiar emotion" when he read the letter from his twenty-six admirers.

Breedlove, the second smallpox case, recovered. A woman who visited him, a Mrs. Humphrey, thought she was immune but caught a slight case of smallpox. She too recovered. For the next several weeks the papers continued their announcements that no new cases had appeared and that people could come and go in safety.

After a while, these messages faded away as smallpox became only a troubling memory. Of the three people who contracted the disease, one had died. However, Milledgeville was for a time scared out of its wits. With courage and dignity, Dr. Tomlinson Fort, acting alone, rose above the hysteria as a true hero of his or any other time.

WILKINSON — A STREET NAMED
FOR A SCOUNDREL

S HORTLY AFTER MOVING TO MILLEDGEVILLE, I was fortunate to go on a tour guided by Dr. Robert Wilson, a history professor at Georgia College & State University. I doubt anyone has ever had contact with Dr. Wilson and not gone away with a new appreciation for history. His enthusiasm for the subject is infectious. This tour was no exception.

The tour ended at the gates to Memory Hill Cemetery. It was raining. Not wanting to let the others on the tour know my ignorance, I waited for them to ask Bob their final questions before scurrying off to their vehicles. Bob and I were left alone standing in the rain. I had just one question to ask but I'd been bursting to ask it for almost an hour.

"Bob, was Wilkinson Street named for James Wilkinson?" His face lit up, as those of you who know him can visualize. With a big grin and eyes shining, he replied, "Yes, it was." I started laughing and said, "that street has to be one of the few things on earth named for that guy!" The rain came down harder as we stood there laughing and talking history. When we finally went our separate ways, after half an hour, we were both very wet. I don't know about Bob, but I had a wonderful time.

Perhaps the story of James Wilkinson is taught locally. I doubt it is mentioned much elsewhere. He never achieved the infamy of a Benedict Arnold, but in his own way he was as sneaky, lying and backstabbing a scoundrel as the United States has ever produced. Moreover, if things had gone his way, he may have outshined Benedict Arnold as a traitor to his country.

During the Revolutionary War, Wilkinson was on General Horatio Gates's staff at the battle of Saratoga. After the victory, Wilkinson was given the pleasant task of rushing the exciting news of victory to the Continental Congress. He stopped along the way to visit his girlfriend for a few days. Congress was a bit upset about the delay—victories were few and far between—but at Gates's urging, Congress made twenty-year-old Wilkinson a brigadier general. This outraged other, more experienced and better qualified officers. Later, Wilkinson's relations with Gates deteriorated to the point where Gates is rumored to have challenged him to a duel.

Washington and his supporters lost all confidence in Wilkinson when he was suspected of being involved in the "Conway Cabal," the conspiracy to replace Washington with

Gates during the war. Later, Wilkinson was made clothier general of the army but resigned due to allegations of corruption. To many, Wilkinson was thought to have cheated his way to the top. But, despite clouds around his actions and his character, he managed to wriggle out of his troubles.

After the Revolutionary War, in the 1780s, Wilkinson went to the Kentucky district. There he worked to promote statehood for Kentucky. During this time, Wilkinson passed from being a rogue to a traitor. He took an oath of allegiance to Spain and received payments for his services.

To the Spanish he was "agent 13." In a complicated series of plans and conspiracies, Wilkinson contrived to separate Kentucky not into a new state in the Union, but as part of a new country in the area west of the Alleghenies. This area was to be under Spanish control.

In 1791, he reentered the small peacetime U.S. Army. Upon the death of Anthony Wayne in 1796, he became the country's highest ranking officer. He was still receiving money from Spain. Around 1805, Wilkinson became involved with Aaron Burr in shadowy plots that may have included separating the new Louisiana Territory from the United States. Plans began to unravel and Wilkinson, without admitting any guilt or association, revealed Burr's plans to President Thomas Jefferson. Burr was then arrested and taken to Richmond, Virginia, for trial. Wilkinson's story was suspicious and he was investigated by a Grand Jury. He escaped indictment by a nine to seven vote.

I cannot help but wonder what thoughts of anger and revenge crossed the mind of Aaron Burr as he passed through Fort Wilkinson, three miles south of Milledgeville in 1807, while under guard, on the way to his trial.

In another tangle with the military court, in 1811, Wilkinson was found not guilty. He had been tried, at the urging of President James Madison, for abuse of his authority. In 1812, his military career came to an end with a badly handled campaign to take Montreal in the War of 1812. He again survived a military inquiry regarding his actions, but he was forced to resign.

Wilkinson, always a shadowy figure, was expert at covering his trail and staying a step ahead of the law. It was not until well into the twentieth century that Spanish documents were located in Cuba and Spain that conclusively proved that, for many years, Wilkinson had been an agent of the Spanish government. For the most part, he was an unsuccessful conspirator, but it was not from a lack of trying. He spent his life in intrigues, always the dishonest, scheming, despicable and self interested scoundrel.

I was wrong when I suggested to Dr. Wilson that Wilkinson Street was one of the few places named for James Wilkinson. Actually, his name is found in many places from Kentucky to New Orleans. Next time you are on our Wilkinson Street or in Wilkinson County in either Georgia or Louisiana, take a moment to remember General James Wilkinson, one of the great schemers of American history, and at least chuckle a little.

THE CONVICTED MURDERER AND THE GEORGIA LEGISLATURE

DOES CHIVALRY PAY? FOR SOME it does.

Recently I came across an instance of the law being twisted beyond anything anyone would have thought possible. It is a strange tale and after being in the dark for over 160 years, it needs to see the light of day at least briefly.

In 1840, in Chattooga County, Georgia, a young man named James Hunter murdered a man named B. Lovejoy. I know nothing of the circumstances of the crime, and those circumstances don't seem to have any bearing on the story. Mr. Hunter was tried, during the October term, in the superior court of Chattooga County and found guilty of murder. He was sentenced to be hanged.

Justice was swift in those days. His date with the hangman was scheduled for December 4. Until that time, he was placed in prison. While in prison, he was visited by his wife. On her last visit to the prison, she and her murderer husband exchanged clothes which enabled the disguised James Hunter to make his escape.

The deception was detected several hours later. The loyal Mrs. Hunter was detained in the prison as an accessory to the prison break of her husband. Somehow, James Hunter learned of his wife's detention in the prison. Not wanting his wife to be confined in the prison, he turned himself in to face the gallows.

One would reasonably conclude that the convicted murderer, James Hunter, would have been watched a bit more closely and hanged on schedule in December, but, such thinking does not take into consideration the Georgia legislature.

The legislators were in session in our State House in Milledgeville, and they took up the matter of James Hunter, convicted murderer. The legislature passed an act to pardon James Hunter. The act states

that from and immediately after the passage of this act, the said James Hunter be, and he is hereby declared to be fully, freely and entirely pardoned, exonerated and discharged from the pains and penalties of his said conviction and sentence, as fully, freely, and entirely as if such conviction and sentence had never taken place, or the offence been committed.

No life in prison. No years behind bars. Not even probation. The convicted murderer, James Hunter, was given a get-out-of-jail-free card on November 21, 1840. The December 19 *Saturday Evening Post* said "the husband was, in this case, worthy of the wife."

What about B. Lovejoy, the man who was murdered? Is there no justice for him? Apparently not. I can't help but wonder what Mr. and Mrs. James Hunter did with the rest of their lives.

THE SCULPTURE BY
ROBERT E. LAUNITZ

IN THE MIDDLE OF THE 1800s, one of the most prestigious sculptors in the United States was Robert E. Launitz of New York City. He mainly specialized in elaborate cemetery monuments for very prominent and wealthy clients. He has been referred to as the father of monumental art in America.

His pieces were horrifically expensive, usually carved out of marble and are fine examples of the carver's art. Most of his work went into cemeteries and monuments of an impressive size. Cemeteries proudly boast when they have a Launitz.

As far as I know, there are only five Launitz works in Georgia. Three of them are in our Memory Hill Cemetery. On the east side, there is the magnificent tombstone of Elizabeth Taylor Jordan, the wife of Green Hill Jordan, who died in 1858. This large monument is made of marble from Carrara, Italy. It contains two fine symbolic sculptures of angels.

The east side also has the large obelisk of the Lamar family. Oddly, the Lamar monument is not elaborately carved, but very simple in design. However, Launitz' name is clearly visible on the east side of the base.

On the west side of the cemetery is the tallest monument in Memory Hill. It marks the grave of Benjamin S. Jordan. Jordan, one of the wealthiest men in the state, died in 1856. This monument is approximately forty feet tall. It has a large cube at the bottom of the square base shaft. At the top of the shaft stands an angel.

The Jordan monument looks a great deal like the Pulaski Monument in Savannah. Launitz created the fifty-five-foot-tall Pulaski Monument in 1853, just a few years before the Jordan Monument. Many of the features are similar besides just the cube base and shaft. On each corner of the cube there is a cannon pointing downward on the Pulaski Monument as a symbol of military loss and mourning. On the Jordan Monument, inverted torches indicate the extinguishing of life as the spirit goes heavenward.

The shaft of each monument is in several pieces. Instead of unsightly horizontal joints on each shaft, there are decorative bands. At the top of both monuments is an elaborate cap. In the case of Pulaski, a statue of liberty holding the flag stands on the cap. Jordan's angel stands with a raised arm and finger pointing toward heaven.

Launitz used this basic design several times. The sixty-three-foot-tall Kentucky War Memorial in Frankfort, Kentucky, was built in 1850 along the same lines: cube base and tall square base shaft with a figure on top.

In Cooperstown, New York (where the Baseball Hall of Fame is located), there is a monument to James Fenimore Cooper. It is a somewhat smaller version of the same design that is only about twenty four feet tall. On the top of this shaft stands Cooper's fictional hero Natty Bumppo with his dog, Hector.

These monuments were not cheap. The one for Pulaski cost $17,000 in 1853, which would be equivalent to over $350,000 in today's dollars.

Next time I go to Washington, DC, I intend to visit the Washington Monument. I'll take the stairs up rather than the elevator. At the 130-foot level, on the east wall, at the eleventh landing, there is an 8-by 5-foot ornate marble plaque carved by Launitz honoring the city of New York. While catching my breath from the climb, I'll admire the carving and remind myself that back home in Milledgeville we have three works by the famous Launitz.

Ty Cobb in Milledgeville

O VER NINETY YEARS AGO, PERHAPS the greatest baseball player of all time, Ty Cobb, played a game in Milledgeville. It was April 1, 1913, when Ty Cobb and his team of all-stars played an exhibition game against Georgia Military College (GMC).

Ty Cobb was holding out for a salary of $15,000 to play for the Detroit Tigers for the 1913 season, which was to begin in a couple of weeks. He was as aggressive in his salary negotiations as he was on the playing field. He told the local reporter, "Right at present I fear that too many believe I play the game for the love of it, but this is not true. . . . It is a business and every man should get as much from his business as is possible."

Cobb knew he was valuable. In the 1912 season, his batting average was a remarkable .409. Almost unbelievably, his average the year before was .420. He would be signed by the Tigers for 1913 and would average "only" .390 for the year. Ty Cobb, "The Georgia Peach," was elected to the Hall of Fame in 1936. His lifetime batting average was .367. He hit over .300 for twenty-three straight years, including three seasons over .400.

Cobb would be joined for the game with GMC by other major league players: Tom McMillan, Jimmy Archer, Ducky Holmes, Nap Rucker, Harry Holland and Ed LaFitte, among others. Unfortunately, I don't have the first names of the GMC ballplayers. Their last names were Nunnally, Ellison, Wilkinson, Lanier, Taylor, Swann, David, Calloway, Bradford, Camp, Gheesling and Harrell.

This was such a big event for Milledgeville that the *Milledgeville News* came out with an extra edition on Monday, March 31, with news about the upcoming game. With a four-column headline proclaiming, "Ty Cobb and His Famous All-Star Baseball Team Will Play Big Game in Milledgeville On Tuesday," the paper set the tone for the extra edition.

Between 2,000 and 2,500 people showed up for the game. That's quite a crowd considering the total population of Milledgeville was only about 4,300 and all of Baldwin County had only about 18,000 people. Descriptions of the game are unclear and contradictory. It seems, however, that Cobb batted third and hit a home run over the right field fence on the first ball pitched to him. There were ground rules in place which gave him only a double. On another at-bat, he stole second base. After one of these stellar plays, he was tagged out as he stepped off the base to bow to the Georgia Normal & Industrial College girls that attended the game "in large numbers." The crowd loved it. Cobb got three hits in the game.

The final score is in doubt. The *Milledgeville News* said that Cobb's team won nine to five. However, the *Atlanta Journal-Constitution* gave the score as ten to five. The Atlanta paper also commented that GMC "batted fine but was guilty of 'bum' base running and fielding." A double play was made by GMC shortstop Lanier, who fielded a hot ground ball.

Whatever the final score, undoubtedly the spectators and the GMC team had a wonderful time. I am sure that the GMC players took home souvenir baseballs, autographs and memories that were treasured throughout their lives.

THE GREAT EARTHQUAKE
OF 1886

A T 9:35 P.M. ON TUESDAY, August 31, 1886, with the sound like a distant railroad locomotive, the windows in Milledgeville rattled as the floors moved up and down. This was no small local trembler. The earthquake was centered near Charleston, South Carolina, and the shocks were felt as far away as Boston, Bermuda and Milwaukee. My grandmother, who experienced this earthquake while in Columbia, South Carolina, told me seventy-five years later how frightened she and others had been.

There was little structural damage in Milledgeville. The State House sustained some cracked walls and one of the chimneys of the McComb Hotel lost some bricks, as did various other chimneys around town. Plaster also fell down in many homes and buildings. The Darien Bank may have suffered the most damage as the walls cracked and bulged out of line.

There were no injuries locally. However, many people were given a good scare. A guest at the McComb Hotel ran into the street during the quake, shouting that everyone should get out of the building. Prudently, his advice was followed. It is said that one lady was told that she had left her room door open, to which she replied, "Oh gracious! No human being would steal anything at such a time as this." The streets of Milledgeville were filled with excited people long into the evening. Some residents experienced a feeling of seasickness caused by the movement of the earth.

There were many stories of religious revivals and church services being held at the time of the earthquake. The participants were all greatly affected by the timing of the quake. Some non-churchgoers were said to have sped to the churches. In Charleston, after the quake, services were held in the rubble.

The scene at the asylum was frightening and came close to becoming a tragedy. An evening entertainment of the "Asylum Dilettanti" was taking place in the amusement hall in the female convalescent building when the quake struck. A sound much like distant thunder was heard and then the building shook and rocked as if it were a ship at sea. Plaster broke from the ceiling and fell onto the crowd. The fifty or sixty people, mostly convalescent patients, "became at once wild with a frenzied panic." With cries and shrieks they rushed to the doors, only to find them locked. Walls and gaslights were swaying as the floor heaved up and down while the screaming press of humanity fought to get the doors open. Finally, attendants were able to unlock the doors and many rushed to the safety of the open air.

Within minutes, Dr. Whitaker came into the room and with "cool heroism" raised his hands in an assuring manner and called for all to remain quiet and stay where they were, confidently telling them they would be safe. Dr. O'Daniel appeared and calmed the fears of patients and guests. He asked two ladies to play a duet on the piano to help divert people from the excitement around them. Soon, Dr. Powell came into the room. His mere presence and dignity had the power to quickly calm the fears, and noise, of the crowd. The building was not badly damaged and no one was injured. The calamity of a panic-driven stampede was avoided.

Charleston was badly damaged—not a building was spared. Large cracks, from which warm water flowed, appeared in the streets. Many buildings were seriously damaged or destroyed. Streets were blocked by the rubble of fallen buildings; fires erupted in the ruins. The population lived in the streets for days, fearing to return to their unstable dwellings. Today, visitors to Charleston are shown the "earthquake bolts" used to stabilize buildings damaged by the 1886 earthquake.

Relief poured into Charleston. Six days after the quake, the *Union Recorder* carried an article describing how people all over the country were scrambling to send aid. Within hours the mayor of Charleston received a dispatch from the mayor of Boston: "Draw on me for $5,000." Silversmiths in Chicago raised $700 in a few days. Donations poured in from all over. However, the *Union Recorder* commented,

what immediately concerns us is, what is Milledgeville going to do? We know that we are somewhat slow in action as a community, but are we to lag behind or do nothing in this matter? Can we leave to our children the legacy of such a blot upon our history? We say emphatically no. Some action must and will be taken and it should not be delayed. We were pleased to hear Frank Mapp read yesterday morning a telegram from P.J. Cline in Macon in which he said "Start a subscription list for Charleston sufferers." Since writing the above Mr. Mapp and Mr. Arthur Carr have been going around among our citizens to receive their contributions.

Two weeks later the newspaper carried an article stating, "the speedy and munificent contributions, of Northern people for the sufferers in Charleston, show that we are one people and that former angry passions have given way to brotherly sympathies," and that "all remaining passions have lost their vehemence in these acts of kindness, which play so happily upon the heartstrings of the people of all sections, upon those who give and those who receive." The article concludes with,

These acts of kindness possess a magnetic influence which draws the people together and in this restoring work, the northern have the advantage of the Southern people in that they are the bestowers of blessings upon the Southern. The Southern, however, have it in their power to do great good in meeting the northern in a spirit of reconciliation and proclaiming with equal sincerity and ardor, that we are all brothers in a restored Union.

The great earthquake of 1886 brought death, misery and destruction to many, but perhaps it helped heal the nation's old wounds, too.

President McKinley's
Visit to Milledgeville

December 19, 1898, was a cold, raw day in Milledgeville. Rain poured down in sheets. The streets were deep in mud and slush. It was the kind of day when everyone gladly stayed indoors. But, today was like no other. The president of the United States was coming to Milledgeville!

The presidential train was to pass through Milledgeville and arrangements had been made for it to stop. Over a thousand people gathered at the depot waiting and listening, for the train. The cadets from the Middle Georgia and Agricultural College, as Georgia Military College was known then, were assembled under arms. As the train came into sight, it was greeted by cadets firing two cannons.

The train had not even come to a halt when the cheering crowd rushed upon it. With cannons booming, the crowd enthusiastically cheering and the Apollo Silver Band playing "Dixie," the president was welcomed to Milledgeville.

The president, a former Union soldier, stood on the platform of his car and spoke to the cheering crowd standing in the pouring rain. He said,

It gives me very great pleasure and honor to meet and greet the citizens of Milledgeville, the old capital of the state of Georgia. In all my journey through your state, I have been received with a warmth of welcome unprecedented, and I assure you that this warm welcome is reciprocated from the bottom of my heart. I am glad to know that once more this country, North and South, all the people of all sections, are united in one purpose, one aim, one hope, and one destiny, under the glorious old banner of the free. And nothing gives me more satisfaction and honor than to feel that as President of this great republic, called by the suffrage of the people, I am permitted to proceed through a nation that is unbroken and can never be broken again.

The cheering crowd then called for Joe Wheeler. Wheeler had been a Confederate general and was well remembered for the exploits of his cavalry. The Spanish-American War had brought Wheeler back into the military, but, this time he would be in command of the U.S. Cavalry in Cuba. His triumphs in Cuba were only a few months in the recent past. However, I suspect that his reputation of thirty-five years earlier was what the crowd really wanted to honor him for. "Fighting" Joe Wheeler spoke a few sentences and then introduced the crowd to his current commander, General William R. Shafter, who bowed his thanks to the crowd.

Dr. George D. Case of Milledgeville handed the president a gift which was unique to Milledgeville. The card attached to it read, "Presented to President William McKinley as a civil war relic, a genuine Joe Brown Pike." These pikes were made during the war and supplied to state troops by then Governor Joseph Brown. While not an effective weapon, they were symbolic of the will of the people never to be conquered. Dr. Case was making the statement, through the gift, that weapons would never again be needed against the president of the United States.

Mayor Horne presented to President McKinley an address written by cadet Captains William McKinley (a local citizen of the same name as the president) and James K. Jordan, which expressed the loyalty of the cadet battalion to the president.

Suddenly, it was over. The train whistle blew, cannons boomed, the band played and the crowd cheered while the president stood on the rear platform, bowing and waving his handkerchief as the train moved out.

THE HISTORY OF
PARSON WEEMS

MASON LOCKE WEEMS, BETTER KNOWN as Parson Weems, considered himself a historian. But, he was far more interested in pleasing people than he was with researching and writing history. His exaggerations and fabrications of fact led one commentator to remark that Weems had "a touch of the confidence man in him."

Weems was born in England in 1759 and ordained by the archbishop of Canterbury in 1784. Ten years later he became a traveling book salesman and author. He wrote sermons and religious tracts. His claim to fame, however, are his books on famous Americans from the Revolutionary period: George Washington, Benjamin Franklin and Francis Marion. In 1800, he wrote *The Life of Washington*, which was extremely popular. To make the book even more popular, Weems added the fictional incident of young George Washington and the cherry tree to the fifth edition in 1806.

In September of 1810, Parson Weems and his mobile bookstore known as the "Flying Library" arrived in Milledgeville. His advertisement proclaims, "In a happy republic, like ours, where for the prize of Fame and Fortune, all start fair and fair alike; where everything depends on merit, and that merit is all dependent on Education, it is hoped that wife and generous parents will need no persuasion to give their children those very great advantages which Books afford. An appropriate Oration on the benefits of Education will be pronounced." His arrival in Milledgeville coincided with the opening of the superior court and also with the opening session of the Georgia legislature.

Weems visited Eatonton and Sparta, but Milledgeville was his base of operations and where he gained his most influential customers. In November, just before he took the Flying Library elsewhere, he was invited to speak before the legislature in the representative chamber. The topic of his talk would be "The Education of Youth."

George Washington and the cherry tree was only one of his many liberties with the truth. In his book on Francis Marion he was supposed to take the work of Marion's friend, General Peter Horry, and put it into book form. Horry was shocked with the result. He wrote Weems, "I requested you would so far alter the work as to make it read grammatically, and I gave you leave to embellish the work, but entertained not the least idea of what has happened…You have carved and mutilated it with so many erroneous statements [that] your embellishments, observation and remarks, must necessarily be erroneous as proceeding from false grounds…Can you suppose I can be pleased with reading particulars of Marion and myself, when I know such never existed?"

Weems's appearance before the legislature was a great success. It prompted an open letter, published in the newspapers, from Governor David Brydie Mitchell to Weems. In it Mitchell said he had just read *The Life of Washington* and also *The Life of General Francis Marion* and these publications had "exalted my opinion of them to still far higher degrees." The governor also commented on "the pains which you have taken in collecting so many very valuable, but hitherto generally unknown, anecdotes of these two noblest champions of American Rights, I pray you to accept my best thanks. And for painting them, with all their virtues and gallant deeds in such glowing colors for the imitation of their young countrymen, I doubt not but you will receive from our citizens that hearty approbation and support which you so well deserve."

Weems must have chuckled when he read that endorsement of his version of "history." It's a shame that General Peter Horry wasn't in Milledgeville to set the record straight. The unknowing public loved Weems's works. *The Life of Washington* for decades outsold every book in the United States except the Bible. It was continuously in print until 1927 and has been reprinted again so it is currently available. Today, however, virtually everyone recognizes Weems's histories for the fiction that they are.

A Tornado Almost Destroys
Milledgeville in 1875

In 1875, with no Doppler radar, TV, radio or tornado/air raid sirens to warn of an approaching tornado, the amount of time to take cover in an emergency was often measured in seconds. It was 1:00 p.m. on a Saturday afternoon when storm clouds were noticed in the western sky. Just a thunderstorm, of course. Suddenly, an hourglass-shaped cloud connecting the ground to the heavens was visible from downtown Milledgeville. The cloud was luminous as though it was lit with a fire, so people rushed into the streets expecting to find a fire. The fire alarm bells in Milledgeville started tolling.

Instead of a fire, the tornado was seen approaching from the northwest. Milledgeville was doomed. Fortunately, the huge tornado turned and passed south of Milledgeville. Just as quickly, it turned again to the northeast, passing north of the Oglethorpe University buildings. It went directly over Midway Cemetery, damaging fencing and trees but not the grave of Reverend Samuel K. Talmadge (the grave of Talmadge was moved and now is in Memory Hill Cemetery), the founder and longtime president of Oglethorpe. The tornado was about three hundred yards wide and cut a path of complete destruction between Milledgeville and Midway.

Witnesses describe it "taking up trees and fences, a house is in its path; quick as thought the house is licked up by the awful monster, another and another, to the number of seven or eight disappear, and the Storm-King has driven past our city and across the river."

Mary, the wife of Thomas Johnson, was "horribly mangled" and died in a few hours. Richard Gause suffered an awful head injury and was killed instantly. The *Union Recorder* reported the grisly story that "a portion of his skull being entirely gone, which was afterwards found half a mile off, and brought to the church when the funeral was progressing." Other people were killed or seriously injured. One child was picked up by the tornado and never found.

The woods all along the tornado's path were covered with household debris. Huge areas of timber in the direct line of the tornado were entirely destroyed. Horses were picked up and seriously injured as they slammed into trees or the ground. One person witnessed the tornado crossing the Oconee River and said that the resulting waterspout was over one hundred feet high and for an instant he was able to see the riverbed. The trees in the area of the crossing were covered with mud. Large numbers of chickens were killed and residents went around picking them up for immediate consumption.

The tornado was not local to Milledgeville. It went all the way from Alabama to South Carolina, cutting a swath of devastation across the entire state of Georgia. In some places, railroad cars were thrown off the tracks. Baldwin County, and particularly Milledgeville, were fortunate in comparison to other locations.

After the storm, the grand jury of the Baldwin superior court appointed a committee to assess the damages. In their report they found that nine people were killed, sixty seriously injured and ninety-four houses blown down. A list was published of the dead and injured. A rough approximation of the dollar amount of the property damage sustained was also listed. In many cases a simple "lost all furniture and clothing" or "lost everything" paints a picture of utter destruction and misery.

A letter to the editor of the *Union Recorder* stated, "several of the cities of Georgia have taken prompt steps to aid the sufferers by the late tornado, while Milledgeville has done nothing. This should not be so." The letter reminded readers that "many of our friends have lost their *all*—have no where to lay their heads—have nothing wherewith to be clothed, and not a mouthful of food to stay the ravages of gnawing hunger. Let His Honor, Mayor [James W.] Herty, bring this matter to the attention of the City Council."

In the same newspaper was a letter from Joseph Lane and E.P. Lane thanking "our citizens, who so kindly assisted both ourselves and Mrs. Wm. H. Lane after the destruction of our property." The letter ends with, "their acts of kindness will be long, long remembered and cherished in the hearts of each of the beneficiaries."

A letter was also published from two lumbermen in Cochran, Georgia, addressed to the mayor of Milledgeville, informing him that a railroad car of lumber from each of their mills was being sent to Milledgeville as a donation.

Disaster relief in the days before federal and state governmental agencies was a far more personal thing than it is today. Help for the most part only came from neighbor helping neighbor. The damages, mostly uninsured, might also be something that the family would never really recover from financially. All that had been accumulated over a lifetime could be blown away and the family, perhaps even physically injured, would have to start over again. No disaster is fun. It wasn't then and it isn't now; but we can be thankful that today we have the benefits of faster communication, far better medical assistance and insurance and governmental help to act as safety nets. The same tornado today would fade in memory sooner thanks to disaster relief avenues in place. If the tornado had not changed course just west of Milledgeville, the entire future of Milledgeville might have been different, too.

ABNER HAMMOND —
THE MAN WITH TWO GRAVES

FEW PEOPLE CAN CLAIM MORE than one grave. Abner Hammond, the Revolutionary War veteran and former Georgia secretary of state, has two tombstones. Each tombstone apparently represents a gravesite.

Hammond lived on the south side of Fishing Creek, east of Elbert Street. Late on the evening of Thursday, July 9, 1829, the sixty-seven-year-old man was riding his horse from Milledgeville to his home. He didn't make it. Fishing Creek was high due to heavy rains and he was apparently swept away and drowned as he attempted to ford the stream. It was a few days before his body was found several miles downstream in the Oconee River.

He was buried on Tuesday, July 14, 1829, with military and Masonic honors. I have searched but unfortunately records from 1829 do not indicate just where he was buried. I presume that he was buried on his property on the south side of Fishing Creek. The story now leaps ahead to August of 1865. Sarah, the wife of Abner Hammond, died. Records do not state where Sarah was buried either, but a tombstone in Memory Hill Cemetery carries an inscription for both Abner and Sarah Hammond. It has been suggested, and seems reasonable, that Abner Hammond was initially buried on his property south of Fishing Creek and later his remains were moved to what became the family plot in Memory Hill. Then, when his wife died, a tombstone was erected for them both in Memory Hill.

The joint tombstone of Sarah and Abner was in place in Memory Hill Cemetery in 1885, and in that year their son, John, died and was buried there. In the article on John Hammond's funeral, the sharp-eyed reporter for the *Union Recorder* mentioned seeing the tombstone for Abner Hammond in the same lot.

We again leap in time to Flag Day, June 14, 1936. The Daughters of the American Revolution unveiled a new government tombstone for Abner Hammond. The unveiling was performed by descendants of Abner Hammond. This new tombstone was not placed in Memory Hill but instead in a field on the south side of Fishing Creek on property that had belonged to Abner Hammond. I presume that this is the location of Abner Hammond's first burial place. I cannot help but wonder how, after the passage of 109 years, it was determined that Hammond was actually buried on the south side of Fishing

Creek, and if he was buried there, where to locate the tombstone. Apparently no one was troubled by the existence of a tombstone for Abner Hammond in Memory Hill Cemetery, which had been there for at least 50 years. So many questions could be easily answered if only good records had been kept in 1829, 1865 and 1936. Perhaps that is the lesson we should learn from this story of the two graves of Abner Hammond.

"The Stars Are Falling!" — The Great Meteor Shower of 1833

Perhaps the most spectacular meteor shower ever recorded occurred in the early morning hours of November 13, 1833. We've all seen meteors streak across the sky. Occasionally, we've seen meteor showers where several meteors can be seen at the same time. I always go outside on those occasions in hopes of seeing an impressive display.

The shower of 1833 tops everything ever seen before or since; it is the stuff of legend. In Milledgeville, we are fortunate to have three newspapers that covered the event. The *Georgia Journal* said it was "the most splendid celestial phenomenon we ever witnessed." Meteors were "incessantly darting in every direction and in such multitudes" that it was "fireworks on a grand scale indeed!" Some of the meteors left trails behind them "that filled the heavens with swords and serpents . . . that were altogether grand to the philosopher and must have been awful and terrible to the superstitious." They "seemed to illuminate the whole heavens."

The *Federal Union* attempted to make a scientific evaluation of the phenomenon asserting that the "brilliant meteors" became "visible at first about one thousand feet above the surface of the ground, and leaving a train of white light, they exploded without noise and vanished when within about two hundred feet." While the reporter's estimates of height and distance are wildly inaccurate, it does give us a good description of what was seen.

The *Federal Union* continued, saying that "the number of meteors defied computation" and that their light "would have enabled a person to read the smallest print." The *Southern Recorder* said "the heavens became illuminated by thousands of shooting stars" in "the most sublime and awful spectacle which nature can present. The blaze was splendid, so as to give the sky the appearance of sunrise."

There were several amusing incidents that took place during the meteor shower, which the papers gleefully reported. A woman and her daughters were kneeling in prayer when a neighbor blew a horn to awaken his neighbors to the spectacular sight. At the sound of the horn those in prayer "prayed with renewed fervency" as they "took this for the last trumpet of the Angel Gabriel."

A man, greatly frightened, looked up to the blazing sky and said, "Well this one thing I do know, escape or not—live long or die soon, I never will drink another drop of liquor."

The *Georgia Journal* commented that "it is to be hoped the falling of the stars may rebound to his advantage in the end."

Of course, the great meteor shower of 1833 was not a local phenomenon. It was seen all over the eastern United States. It coincided with the Mormons being driven out of Jackson County, Missouri. They awoke to the spectacular display and saw it as a sign from God. A mob forming to further harass the Mormons got the same idea and disbanded.

It's impossible to calculate the number of meteors visible but estimates range into the hundreds of thousands per hour. Each November I hope that we will again be presented with a spectacular Leonid meteor shower comparable to that of 1833.

ABNER HAMMOND'S FIGHT
WITH GOVERNOR JOHN CLARK

IN 1822, THERE WAS A MAJOR confrontation between Governor John Clark and Secretary of State Abner Hammond, an aging Revolutionary War veteran. Political power, power of the press, physical strength, intimidation, fists, angry accusations and even bloodshed combined in an event that kept the newspapers buzzing for many weeks.

Events began quietly with Abner Hammond leaving Milledgeville on July 11 on a trip to the Georgia seacoast in an effort to improve his health. He left his office in the charge of his senior clerk, Thomas H. Crawford. As was customary, Hammond left Crawford with some blank forms, as well as a power of attorney, signed by Hammond, which allowed Crawford to handle affairs in Hammond's absence.

John Clark left on about the same date for a trip to Athens. Clark returned to Milledgeville on Saturday, August 10. On Monday, Clark declared the secretary of state's office had been vacated and that a man of the governor's choosing, Simon Whitaker, was appointed secretary of state. The governor's proclamation stated the grounds for this action was Hammond's absence "for some time past . . . without the permission or knowledge of the Executive," and that "it is very uncertain when he will return." Further, the governor contended that, "there being no law or resolution of the Legislature authorizing a deputy to discharge the duties of said office, it is therefore considered by the Executive that the office which he filled as Secretary, is thereby vacated."

On Tuesday, August 13, Governor Clark, along with one of his secretaries and Simon Whitaker, went to the secretary of state's office, informed Thomas Crawford that Whitaker was taking over the position of secretary of state, and demanded the records, books and keys to the office. Thomas Crawford firmly refused and said that he would give up the office to Abner Hammond and no one else. The governor then threatened him with arrest. Crawford stood firm in his refusal. The governor then told Crawford that he would have him physically thrown out of the State House. Crawford refused to leave or turn over his keys and records. The governor left. Whitaker went to a justice of the peace to get an arrest warrant.

The justice of the peace refused to give an arrest warrant, as he could find no law that authorized it. Whitaker then returned to the secretary of state's office with a carpenter. He told the carpenter to remove the lock from the door and replace it with another. Crawford convinced the carpenter to leave the lock alone. Whitaker then went to the executive office and returned with a Mr. Burch, one of the governor's secretaries. This time the carpenter started to work on the lock while the door was being held by Burch. At that point, "a battle ensued between Mr. Burch and Mr. Crawford, in which, it seems, Mr. Whitaker took a hand." The combatants were separated by people in the hallway of the State House, who came running at the sound of the conflict. Burch was bleeding slightly. The governor then appeared "in a violent passion" and ordered that the carpenter change the lock. Crawford had lost possession of the secretary of state's office.

The newspapers took up this story while strongly editorializing regarding the personalities and legalities involved in the violent ousting of the secretary of state. The *Southern Recorder* commented that "throughout the whole of this business, Governor Clark has laid aside that dignity and respect which belonged to his office, and has acted in a violent, lawless, and outrageous manner to which only the history of his own life can furnish a proper parallel." That's pretty strong.

There was nothing in the Georgia constitution or in any law that allowed the governor to remove an absent secretary of state and appoint a replacement. The governor at that time was not elected by popular vote but rather by the legislature. The secretary of state was also elected by the legislature. Their offices were entirely independent. Hammond did not have to report to Clark in any manner. Also, it was common practice for absent officeholders to select a member of their staff to conduct business while they were away. In fact, the governor had done it as recently as the previous day when he had one of his secretaries sign documents in his name.

For weeks the newspapers were full of angry editorials and letters to the editor. The letters were anonymous and signed by such names as "Common Sense." Several long pro-Clark letters were written by "Plain Truth" and "Friend to Truth." It was generally accepted that these letters were written by Governor Clark himself.

In a letter to the legislature, Governor Clark said of Hammond, "for years he has been more inattentive to his duties than any officer attached to the State House. He has often been unable from various causes to sign his name, and frequently got some one of the young men in the office to do it for him. If this is allowed of, he need never go into his office."

The governor didn't have a leg to stand on. The case was taken to the courts and the ruling came down in favor of Abner Hammond, who was then allowed to reassume his office and function. In his long ruling, the judge commented on the various legal aspects of the case and gave the governor nothing to be happy about. In one place he said, "It is no argument to say, that no Governor would ever abuse his privilege in the manner suggested, the form and principles of our Government never intended to place it in his power; for the people of this country are too well informed not to know, that all men love power, and that when interest or passion has the ascendancy, they are too apt 'to feel might and forget right.'"

This incident received attention all across the country. The *New York Statesman* referred to the episode as a "most unwarrantable usurpation." The paper continued, "we can not perceive, that he had the shadow of right or legitimate authority, to remove Col. Hammond and appoint Mr. Whitaker. The passionate manner in which he executed this unauthorized measure, is not very creditable to Governor Clark, either as a man or a magistrate."

Governor John Clark was not elected governor for another term. After having served twelve years as secretary of state, Abner Hammond was not elected for another term, either. The old Revolutionary War veteran had fought, and won, his last battle.

CHATHAM STREET

IN 2003, THE MILLEDGEVILLE CITY COUNCIL approved changing the name of Chatham Street to Earnest Byner Street. This change was made to recognize Earnest Byner's devotion of countless hours to volunteering at Boys & Girls Clubs. Byner has become an excellent role model for children. It's a good idea and I think a street should be named for him.

As the street signs come down and the old name fades in memory, I'm sure that some people will wonder who or what "Chatham" is or was. It's an unusual name, but it is a name that is encountered frequently in the areas of the United States that were once colonies of England.

The name comes from the Englishman William Pitt, "The Elder," who was to become the Earl of Chatham. He was born November 15, 1708, in London, England, and died May 11, 1778, in Kent. Before he became an earl he was known as the "Great Commoner." He was elected to Parliament as a young man and quickly rose to become a leader in the House of Commons. As a powerful politician, he helped forge England into a great power and started the growth of the British empire.

William Pitt and King George III disagreed continually. Pitt was forced to resign in 1761, but continued his attacks on the King's policies of taxation of the American colonies. This made Pitt very popular in America. In 1766, Pitt was made prime minister and also given the title of the Earl of Chatham. Despite debilitating poor health, he continued to attack the British government's American policy. He was considered in America as the colonies' best friend and spokesman in the British government. He urged major concessions on every American grievance, only stopping short of advocating complete independence for the colonies.

In 1777, while the war in America raged, he said, "If I were an American, as I am an Englishman, while a foreign troop was landed in my country I never would lay down my arms,—never! never! never!" Such sentiments made him very popular in the newly declared independent colonies.

He also was an advocate of law and the rights of the common man. He said, "the poorest man may in his cottage bid defiance to all the force of the Crown. It may be frail, its roof may shake; the wind may blow through it; the storms may enter, the rain may enter, but the King of England cannot enter; all his forces dare not cross the threshold of the ruined tenement!"

This was the man, as the Earl of Chatham, whose memory was preserved on the Chatham Street sign. While the name of the street has changed, there is still a place to remind us of William Pitt, the Earl of Chatham: Pittsburgh, Pennsylvania.

THOMAS PETTERS CARNES—
REVOLUTIONARY WAR SOLDIER

THOMAS PETTERS CARNES WAS BORN in Maryland in 1762. He died in Milledgeville in 1822 and lies in Memory Hill Cemetery. His gravestone misspells his name as "Peters" when his name actually is "Petters" and lists his military service as "Georgia Troops" when in fact he was colonel of a Maryland regiment.

Despite its faults, this gravestone marks the burial place of a Patriot, Georgia politician and lawyer. After the Revolutionary War, Carnes moved to Franklin County, Georgia, where he was elected to the Georgia legislature and practiced law beginning in the late 1780s. There is some indication that he was involved in the Yazoo Land Fraud of 1795, in which legislators were bribed into selling huge tracts of land to speculators. However, he was reelected several times. He was also selected to be a judge of the superior court of the northern circuit of Georgia.

In 1806, the Georgia legislature selected Carnes, along with two other men, to be the commissioners to determine the location of the thirty-fifth degree of latitude that separates Georgia from North Carolina and Tennessee. The surveyors had troubles of various sorts, including problems with their equipment. Errors crept into their calculations and measurements. As a result, the survey line runs about four miles south of the actual thirty-fifth degree line, thus making Georgia slightly smaller than it would have been if the boundary had been on the actual thirty-fifth degree line. Tennessee and North Carolina recognized the boundary as surveyed, rather than the thirty-fifth degree line as it should have been. When the mistake was uncovered, Georgia futilely sought to have the boundary line changed.

Four miles doesn't seem like anything to worry about, except when you consider that most of Chattanooga, Tennessee, would be in Georgia had the line been drawn correctly.

Thomas Petters Carnes died in Milledgeville on May 5, 1822, and was buried in a place called the "Old Cemetery." The location of that cemetery has been lost. At some time about seventy-five years ago, his remains were apparently moved to Memory Hill and the incorrectly marked stone put up in his memory. We should remember him, too. He may have mishandled the thirty-fifth degree line, and been involved in the Yazoo Fraud, but he was a well-respected judge. He also stood up when it counted—in the American Revolution. For that alone he deserves to be remembered.

Georgia Normal
and Industrial College's
Forgotten Tragedy

WHEN WE VISIT A CEMETERY we often remember people who lived full lives, achieved goals and witnessed stirring events. However, there are some who never had the opportunity to reach their potential, who died just as the door to their adult life was opening. Mary F. Howard was one of these. For over one hundred years she lay, forgotten by the world, in an unmarked grave in Memory Hill.

Mary, or Pansy as she was called by her friends, was the first student to die while attending Georgia Normal and Industrial College, now called Georgia College & State University. In perfect health, she had entered the sophomore class in September 1896. A month later, on a Sunday afternoon, she became sick. Suffering from dysentery, she grew weaker and weaker as the days slipped past.

She was the seventeen-year-old daughter of Gordon Howard of Wilkinson County. Her mother had died a few years earlier and Pansy lived the last few years in Macon with her uncle, the Honorable S.A. Reid, a prominent lawyer and member-elect to the next Georgia legislature. Her teachers said that she was a remarkably bright and good-looking girl with tremendous potential.

After a week of increasing weakness, she died in the early hours of Saturday, October 10, 1896. Her father, uncle, a brother Gordon Howard and Dr. George Crawford, another uncle, were at her bedside.

The funeral took place from the Baptist church the same afternoon. At that time the Baptist church was located on North Wayne Street. The girls at GN&I College were not allowed to leave the premises except for special occasions. Pansy's funeral was one such event. The entire student body of over three hundred girls, wearing college uniforms and mourning badges, marched to the church and then to Memory Hill Cemetery.

Pansy had once been a student at Middle Georgia Military and Agricultural College, the early name of Georgia Military College. Six of her friends from there acted as her pallbearers. Her sobbing classmates covered her grave with flowers.

Apparently her family never wanted or was able to put up a tombstone in her memory. For the next 105 years, her grave was unmarked and she was forgotten. Then, in 2001, through the efforts of Floride Gardner, a marble marker was placed on her grave. After more than a century she has now been remembered.

Two Memory Hill
Mysteries

I HAVE BEEN ASKED WHO WOULD be the two most mysterious people in Memory Hill Cemetery. I certainly can't vouch for all of the thousands of souls buried there, but two men stand out in my mind as being mysterious to some extent.

The first man is a mysterious stranger. He came to Milledgeville on August 24, 1870, and registered at the Milledgeville Hotel (which was on the northeast corner of Wayne and Greene Streets) under the name of Frank Hamilton. He gave his address as Lynchburg, Virginia.

Hamilton's occupation was piano repairer and tuner. He went about his business for two weeks without anything unusual taking place. However, he soon contracted a "chill" at the private boarding house of a Mr. Nailor. The disease ebbed and flowed but within a few days became quite serious. He received medical treatment to no avail from Dr. Case.

As he grew weaker, it became apparent to Hamilton that he was going to die. On what was to become his deathbed, Hamilton said that his name was not really Frank Hamilton. He said he actually was George Berry, the son of John Berry of Wrexham, England, and that he was twenty-six years old.

On September 19, George Berry died of "bilious fever," without saying why he was traveling under an assumed name or giving the name of any friend or relation to contact. The City of Milledgeville buried him in Memory Hill Cemetery. He lies in an unmarked grave at an unknown location within the cemetery.

The second man isn't a mystery himself. What is somewhat mysterious is the story about him that has been repeated countless times. I am referring to Daniel Lyman of Rhode Island. Apparently, for many years, visitors to Memory Hill have been shown his grave and told about how he was engaged to be married to a Milledgeville girl. Due to unforeseen circumstances, he was delayed in getting to Milledgeville for quite some time. When he finally got here, he discovered that his girl had married someone else. He then, it is said, went to the cemetery and hanged himself. A ghoulish twist to the story is that Lyman was buried beneath the cedar tree where he hanged.

There is no truth to the story. Daniel Lyman died after a "short and severe illness" on August 4, 1822, at the age of twenty-seven. He was buried with Masonic and military honors. He had not committed suicide. He also had not just arrived in Milledgeville. He was a merchant who was well established at least as early as March 1819. His obituary said that he had "many friends in this place who regret his loss." Regrettably I have no information about any females in his life.

Why this young man has had the misfortune of being associated with suicide and an unsuccessful love affair 180 years after his death is a mystery I cannot explain.

CANNONS CAN BE DANGEROUS

IT WOULD SEEM PERFECTLY OBVIOUS that the firing of cannons can be dangerous to the people firing them. Historically, cannons have been used during ceremonial occasions for hundreds of years. Their booming voices add military splendor, as well as fire and smoke, and combine to add an emphasis to special occasions that cannot be matched, except perhaps by a flyover of fighter aircraft.

Fighter aircraft were not available for celebrations in Milledgeville in the 1800s, so cannon fire was the choice when great impact was desired. As the capital, Milledgeville hosted several spectacular occasions which saw cannons in operation.

Cannons of this period were of the muzzle-loading variety. In the simplest terms, they were loaded from the muzzle with a bag of gunpowder, followed by a wad of paper in place of the military projectile. The charge was lighted by a fuse, or match or firing apparatus at the breech end, which allowed a flame to go through the touchhole to reach the main powder charge. The result was the cannon being fired.

After the firing of the cannon, the bore of the cannon was swabbed out with a lamb's wool tool while an artilleryman pressed his thumb, covered by a leather pad, over the touchhole. The idea was to extinguish any particles or sparks that may still be burning within the barrel of the cannon. This was very important, for if the next powder charge was inserted into a barrel containing live sparks, the cannon would immediately fire with potentially disastrous results.

When General Lafayette came to Milledgeville in 1825, the town went to the greatest lengths to celebrate the occasion. There was great feasting, military parades, speeches, toasts, drinking and the firing of cannons. Many military units came to town to take part in the celebration. The state arsenal was in Milledgeville and cannons were supplied to signal the arrival of Lafayette as well as to punctuate various events.

A huge feast was prepared and the assembled crowd was seated at long tables on the State House grounds. Needless to say, the sight of General Lafayette, a hero of the Revolution, was the highlight of the day. Coming in a close second was an accident involving a cannon. The cannons had been firing in celebration when suddenly a huge explosion took place. A man was seen being thrown into the air. It seems that the sleeve of one of the artillerymen had caught fire. The man, unaware of his smoldering sleeve, reached into the ammunition box for another cartridge of gunpowder and set off all the charges at once.

The man was horribly burned "black as a cinder" on his face, chest and arms. He died the next day. Several other men were also burned but they survived the ordeal.

Twenty years later, President Andrew Jackson died. A large ceremony took place on July 16, 1845, in Milledgeville to honor the fallen former general and leader. Cannons were fired. I wonder how many people attending the event, upon hearing the booming cannons, thought of the horrible scene caused by the exploding cartridges in 1825.

Cannons boomed on the State House grounds. Suddenly, a cannon boomed out of sequence. It had gone off prematurely. With much shouting and screaming a crowd formed around the artillery piece. Two artillerymen were injured. John Haas was slightly injured and James Allaman was severely injured. Allaman's hand was shredded—he had been loading the cannon when a spark remaining in the barrel of the cannon had ignited the charge. The firing of the cannon occurred while his hand was directly in front of the muzzle as he rammed the cartridge down the barrel.

James Allaman died the same day. He rests today in Memory Hill under a fine marble stone that reads that he died "from an accidental discharge of a cannon at the funeral obsequies of General Jackson. Honest, mirthful and beloved, he acquired the title of 'Crockett,' it lives in his memory."

"Crockett" may be a reference to Davy Crockett or to something else. Unfortunately, I have no idea what the significance may have been. James Allaman's death may live in our memory but the meaning of "Crocket" has been lost.

The day following this tragedy, the *Georgia Messenger*, a Macon newspaper, reprinted the 1841 instructions for properly firing a cannon as recommended by the secretary of war. This printing was not in response to the accident in Milledgeville, but rather because "the fourth of July is frequently attended with serious accidents arising from the firing of cannon." Perhaps, if the article had been printed the previous week, the accident could have been avoided.

"I Have Seen the Giraffe!"

EVERYONE LOVES A CIRCUS. THIS was as true in nineteenth century Milledgeville as it is today. Newspaper accounts say the "quiet city of Milledgeville" was "somewhat aroused" on Saturday evening, March 28, 1868, when a train unexpectedly pulled up to the station carrying a circus.

This circus had been struggling to the point of being literally bogged down in mud in parts of the state "destitute of both money and provisions." To survive, the circus chartered a train to bring them to Milledgeville, where they hoped to recruit employees, get their wagons repaired at the penitentiary and raise some money through performances. Citizens were exhorted to "get out your dimes and go to the circus." A clown by the name of Charles Covelli was described as being one of the best clowns in America.

The following year, in June, "Col. C.T. Ames' World Famed New Orleans Menagerie, Circus and Aviary" arrived, by pre-arrangement. It featured "more beautiful ladies, more accomplished artists, more brilliant feats, more trained animals, more schooled equines and more gorgeous trappings." What I would really have liked to have seen, however, was "The Grand Street Procession!" which claimed to "present the unheard of spectacular novelty of letting lions and tigers loose in the grand retinue." Plus "other wonders no less attractive." Lions and tigers walking down Hancock Street. That must have been something to see. It would have been wonderful for us if someone had been there with a camera.

In addition to the wild animals walking through town, the circus also featured Mademoiselle Cardonna, "a very fascinating and graceful lady" who was an expert equestrienne and tightrope performer. The Holland Brothers were acrobats. The "handsome and daring" Mademoiselle Eugenie "performed wonderful feats in the den of lions."

In 1869, many people had been to a circus or at least knew something about them. Thirty years earlier, a "stupendous exhibition" came to Milledgeville that brought beasts that were probably new to everyone. The collection included antelopes, gazelles, ibex and a giraffe. The animals were obtained in "the remote and hitherto unexplored regions of Central Africa, far beyond the haunts of civilized man." These animals were being brought to Milledgeville "after five years of perilous labor, great privation, and boundless cost." Admission was fifty cents, with children under ten years of age and servants at half price.

It was suggested, as an added incentive at the time, that "it may be worth while to be able in after times to say 'I have seen the Giraffe!'" The giraffe, indeed, must have been quite a sight on the streets of Milledgeville. I wish I'd seen it.

LINCOLN STREET

THE NAMING OF LINCOLN STREET in Milledgeville has at times been a puzzle to the citizenry. The most well-known Lincoln in history is, of course, Abraham Lincoln, but Abe cannot have been the source of the name of the street, as the street was named long before anyone had heard of Abe Lincoln.

The street actually was named for Benjamin Lincoln, a well-known Revolutionary War general, at the time of the establishment of Milledgeville in the very early 1800s. General Lincoln was born in Massachusetts on January 24, 1733. He was one of the many amateur military men who surfaced to serve in the Revolution. Before the war, he was a farmer, magistrate, representative in the legislature and a colonel of militia. He had no formal training in the military, and the militia at the time was mostly a social organization. His knowledge of military affairs can be assumed to be minimal.

He played a small part in the battle of White Plains, near New York City in 1776. In 1777, he was sent by George Washington to command the New England militia. At the battle of Saratoga, in October of that year, he was wounded by a musket ball in the left ankle. This wound would trouble him for the rest of his life. It caused his left leg to be two inches shorter than his right leg.

After ten months recuperating from his wound, Lincoln returned to service. In September of 1778, he was appointed by Congress to the command of the Southern Department, part of which was Georgia and South Carolina. His base of operations was in Charleston. He made an attempt to capture Savannah from the British in 1779 and laid siege to the city with the aid of the French troops and fleet of Admiral Count d'Estaing. However, he was unable to prevail and when the French abandoned the campaign he retreated back to Charleston.

In 1780, British Lieutenant General Henry Clinton launched an offensive against Charleston. He blockaded Charleston on the sea side with his fleet. Clinton then advanced on Charleston with his army. Benjamin Lincoln barricaded Charleston in hopes of withstanding the siege. It was a hopeless situation from the start. The British dug trenches and worked their way closer and closer to the American defenses until the British cannons were a stone's throw from the American lines. With the end in sight, many of the local Charleston citizens, as well as the militia, petitioned Lincoln to surrender so the city would be spared. They went so far as to threaten that if Lincoln attempted to evacuate across the Ashley or Cooper Rivers, they'd open the gates and let the British in to attack his rear.

Benjamin Lincoln surrendered on May 12. It was a disastrous defeat for the Patriot forces: 3,465 officers and enlisted men of the Continental army, as well as about 2,000 militia, were surrendered. In addition, huge quantities of arms were lost to the Patriots. It was the largest surrender of American forces until Bataan in 1942 during World War II.

In October of 1780, General Lincoln was exchanged and rejoined Washington's army. He was assigned to command troops in the New York area. In October of 1781, British General Charles Cornwallis was forced to surrender at Yorktown. Due to illness, Cornwallis could not attend the surrender ceremony. Legend tells us that Cornwallis's second in command offered his own sword to Washington during the ceremony. Washington refused to accept it and instead allowed Benjamin Lincoln to accept the sword as Cornwallis had forced Lincoln to surrender his sword at Charleston. The truth is that Washington did not accept the offered sword as the officer was not of the same rank as Washington. He properly had General Lincoln receive the sword from the British officer of the same rank.

After the war, Lincoln returned to Massachusetts. He was chosen to negotiate a treaty with the Penobscot Indians. In 1787, he commanded the militia that put down Shays' Rebellion. He was also elected lieutenant governor. He became a member of the state convention that ratified the United States Constitution. He was a member of the Massachusetts Historical Society and the American Academy of Arts and Sciences for which he wrote scientific papers. He died May 9, 1810, in Massachusetts.

While Benjamin Lincoln may not have had as memorable a career as Abraham Lincoln, he did enjoy a full and active life in the formative years of the United States. It is good that we have a Lincoln Street to remind us of him.

MONTGOMERY STREET

I WAS PERSUADED THAT I SHOULD write a column about the origin of the name Montgomery Street when I asked my wife if she knew for whom Montgomery Street was named. She had responded, tongue in cheek, that it must be named for the World War II British field marshal, Bernard Law Montgomery.

Actually, the street was named in honor of the Revolutionary War Patriot Richard Montgomery. Montgomery was born in Ireland on December 2, 1736. He joined the British army at the age of eighteen and intended to make the military his career. As an officer, he fought in the British army, along with the colonists, in the French and Indian War. After the war, he returned to England.

In 1773, after deciding that he would not be promoted in the British army, he sold his commission and returned to America. He married Janet Livingston, of a prominent New York family, and became a farmer. In May 1775, he was made a delegate to the First Provincial Congress in New York City. The following month he was made a brigadier general in the Continental army.

He was second in command, under General Philip Schuyler, on the expedition to Canada in the fall of 1775. Soon Schuyler fell ill and Montgomery took command. Montgomery took his army north from Fort Ticonderoga following Lake Champlain to the St. Lawrence River, where he planned to attack Montreal. He had a force of only a few hundred men but Montreal was not well defended and surrendered.

Montgomery led his men down river to Quebec where he joined forces with those of Colonel Benedict Arnold. Unlike Montreal, Quebec was heavily fortified. The city could not be taken by siege as it was winter and Quebec was well stocked with food. The Americans were suffering from effects of the weather, and shortages of food, ammunition and medical supplies. Smallpox was ravaging the American army. To make matters even worse, the enlistments of the American soldiers were about to expire.

Montgomery and Arnold conceived a bold plan. While the defenders of the city were distracted by a diversion on one side, Arnold and Montgomery were to lead their men, in the hours before dawn on December 31 during a snowstorm, through the narrow winding streets of a portion of the city. Arnold and Montgomery took separate routes through the streets, then joined forces for the final assault on the main part of Quebec. The chances for success were very slim.

Leading his men through twisting streets, Montgomery met an obstacle. In the dim light and blizzard conditions, he saw a two-story blockhouse in his path. Leaving his men fifty yards behind, he, along with four officers and thirteen men, assaulted the silent blockhouse. When they were within a few feet of the blockhouse, the defenders fired cannons and muskets at point-blank range. Montgomery was killed instantly along with several of his men. The survivors fled. Benedict Arnold's attack met a similar fate. Arnold was severely wounded leading an attack and was carried back with the retreating Americans. The assault on Quebec had failed.

Richard Montgomery was buried with full military honors in Quebec. The governor, lieutenant governor, the city council of Quebec and the officers of the garrison attended the burial. In 1818, General Montgomery's remains were removed from Quebec and reburied at St. Paul's Chapel in New York City.

This brave man is remembered by the seventeen states, including Georgia, which named counties in his honor. In Milledgeville, we can be proud of having a street named for Richard Montgomery.

Stories Behind
the Zinc Tombstone of
John Sherrod Thomas

In Memory Hill Cemetery there is one tombstone that is like none of the others. It's not taller, fancier or more expensive than any other tombstone. The reason it is unusual is because it is made of zinc. Zinc tombstones are found all over the United States but are far less common than any other material. The zinc tombstone in Milledgeville's cemetery belongs to John Sherrod Thomas.

The zinc (sometimes called "white bronze") markers are a bluish gray in color and are made of cast zinc. They are hollow. Inscriptions or designs do not lose their sharpness due to weathering as is the case with other materials. Unfortunately, these tombstones are very brittle. When bumped by lawnmowers or falling tree branches the zinc markers will easily snap off. That is the case with the marker of Thomas's wife, Eliza. Her marker has broken off and is missing.

John Sherrod Thomas was the oldest man living in Baldwin County, nearly 102 when he died in 1881. He was born in 1779 on Rocky Creek in Hancock County. Long life seems to follow his family. His mother died at the age of 109. His father, a Revolutionary War veteran, died at the age of 97. It is said that a slave of his father, named Jim, died at the age of 112.

In 1806, Thomas was commissioned by the governor as captain of a volunteer company that was called out a few times to defend against local Indian troubles. In the War of 1812, he was a lieutenant of artillery in the militia company commanded by Captain Jett Thomas. After a year of service, Jett Thomas resigned and John Thomas took over as captain.

John Thomas led an active life in both business and religious affairs. In 1841, the state legislature acted to incorporate the wardens and vestry of St. Stephen's Church. John Thomas was one of the vestrymen. In 1845, he was judge of the inferior court. In 1854, he was one of the men who assisted in the incorporation of the Southern Central Agricultural Society of Georgia. In the 1840s and 1850s, he was director of the Central Bank of Georgia. In 1858, he was one of the incorporators of the Cotton Planter's Convention of the State of Georgia.

He was on friendly terms with the local Indians. When business caused him to carry large sums of cash, they would escort him for his protection.

During the Civil War, Thomas had a contract to provide the government with brandy and whiskey. He would not tolerate speculators buying his product to withhold and sell at a later time for enormous profits. Nor would he allow any employee to defraud the government. He would throw speculators off his property, but any Confederate soldier passing by would receive a meal and provisions to carry with him on his travels.

Thomas would turn over the wool from his four hundred sheep to the women who made it up into cloth and clothing for the soldiers. A few months before the end of the war, when the result was inevitable, Thomas sold $40,000 worth of cotton and invested it in Confederate bonds.

In 1866, Dr. Benjamin Aspinwall White died. He did not want a monument. Instead, he asked his close friend John Thomas to plant an acorn at his grave. The magnificent oak tree at Dr. White's grave, in Memory Hill, is a wonderful monument to Dr. White, but it is also a monument to his friendship with John Thomas.

The last few years of his life, John Thomas was confined to his house in Midway. The cause of his death is officially listed as "old age." His funeral took place from St. Stephens Episcopal Church on a cold and damp day in January 1881. Despite the weather, his remains were followed to Memory Hill by a large number of his friends.

Medieval Knights Vie for Love and Beauty in Milledgeville

It was February 1871. Crowds of spectators from all over the city and county came to witness one of the greatest spectacles of Milledgeville. The tournament was a day-long festival featuring mounted knights and their ladies fair, each suitably dressed for the occasion. The knights, wearing "gay and glittering" costumes, had practiced their riding for weeks. After the contests, a splendid ball was to be held at the Milledgeville Hotel.

At 10:00 a.m. the knights formed in Hancock Street. West's brass band played stirring martial music to add to the pageantry. At the command, they proceeded, in column, down Wayne Street, turning onto Greene Street, then to Liberty Street, where the tournament would take place.

The judges of the event were Adolph Joseph, W. Williamson and J.W. Herty, who viewed the events from the judges' platform. As in tournaments in medieval England, the commander of the knights exchanged military courtesies with the judges. Then, Miller Grieve Jr. reported to the throng that the knights were ready to enter the lists.

Rather than jousting, where riders rode toward each other with lances, these more modern knights raced their steeds while trying to pick up a suspended ring with the end of the lance or sword. Other trials were run for time alone. Bugle calls punctuated the start of each event.

Each participant took on a special name for the occasion. Mark Johnson was the Knight of the Burning Hand; J.M. Whitaker, Knight of the Flaming Heart; Hershel V. Sanford, Richard Coeur de Lion; Ed Bayne, Knight of the Golden Horse Shoe; and Richard Lamar, Knight of the Flaming Sword, to name a few.

The riding was superb. The knights were described as riding their steeds with grace and ease while skillfully using their weapons. It must have been quite a sight—huge cheering crowds, blaring of bugles and the brass band, with knights in complete costume charging down a dirt Liberty Street.

These men were not riding solely for the sake of the fair ladies. The prizes were significant. First place went to Ed Bayne, Knight of the Golden Horse Shoe, who received a life-size portrait of General R.E. Lee. A service of silver went to Thomas West, Knight of Warwick, for second place. The third place prize, a pair of silver spurs, went to Mark Johnston, Knight of the Burning Hand.

That evening, the ball at the Milledgeville Hotel was "one of the largest and most brilliant assemblages ever seen in Milledgeville," according to the *Southern Recorder*. The knights, each accompanied by the lady of his choice, assembled upstairs in the hallway of the hotel. At 8:00 p.m. they formed a procession to the ballroom.

The Queen of Love and Beauty, Fanny Goddard, was crowned by the champion, Ed Bayne. Maggie Whitaker, First Maid of Honor was crowned by Thomas West. Second Maid of Honor, a Miss Burnet of Sparta, was crowned by Mark Johnston. After the coronation, the ball proceeded. The tournament and ball were described as "undoubtedly a most complete and brilliant success."

But, that is not the end of the story of the tournament and ball. A month later, the entire program was repeated. This time the knights would also shoot pistols and there was a bar for their noble steeds to jump. Competition was keen but the number of spectators was fewer than the previous tournament.

Dr. J.C. Whitaker won first prize, which was a saddle and bridle. A pair of Derringers went to George Duncan for second place. George Harris won a silver cup for third place.

As the *Southern Recorder* commented at the time, "Taken altogether, Milledgeville is hard to beat on Tournaments and Balls." I think few could disagree.

THE OLD CAPITOL
BASE BALL CLUB OF 1871

THE EARLIEST EVIDENCE OF BASEBALL being played in Milledgeville seems to be lost in the mists of time. Apparently the very early games, before 1871, were played by the fire companies. In the fall of 1870, interested people met to organize a "base ball club." It was suggested that should a fire occur, the base ball club should act jointly with the fire department in fighting the fire. This probably was in response to the poor numbers of volunteers for the fire departments at the time.

In the spring of 1871, the base ball club was organized and eager to take to the field. Miller Grieve Jr. was elected president. Announcements appeared in the newspapers seeking players. Players and spectators were looking forward to the first games. A "fine ground" was located and practices were taking place. The ball field was located on the Oconee river bottom where it was flat and had plenty of room. In fact, the field was huge. It was three hundred yards wide and five hundred yards long, "thus affording ample room for the most miraculous exploits with a ball and bat." It also meant that there was no outfield fence. Batters would have to run out their home runs.

The principle Milledgeville team was the "Old Capitol," which perhaps was the first usage of the term so common in Milledgeville and Baldwin County today. The games were filled with action. In one game the "Scrubs" beat "Old Capitol" 31 to 21. In another, the score was 24 to 25. Until 1885, pitching was underhand with a stiff arm; no snapping of the wrist or elbow was allowed. This contributed to a large number of hits and runs.

The Macon "Central City" base ball club challenged the Old Capitols to a game. A potential problem arose. The ball field was underwater due to recent rains causing the river to rise. The location of the ball field was changed to the State House square, where it became known simply as the Ball Ground.

Central City was a more experienced team and had practiced more. The Old Capitols played well but not well enough. They lost by a score of 39 to 12. The Old Capitols were Napier, Grieve, Denton, Sallie, Orme, Whiddon, Compton, Wilson and Barrow. Unfortunately, their first names are not specified. There were more men in the club than just these, however. One of them was named Riddle, who I suspect as being A.J. Riddle, a photographer who took photographs of the teams.

In the evening, the Old Capitol "base ballists" hosted a ball for the Macon team at the Milledgeville Hotel. Unfortunately, the Milledgeville ladies were not notified in time so few showed up. Future games were better publicized and even attracted a band to play during the games.

Eatonton was a favorite opponent and several games were played between the Oconee Base Ball Club of Eatonton and Old Capitol. For one game, the players from Eatonton arrived by train at 2:00 p.m. dressed in new uniforms. It is not clear if these uniforms replaced "old" uniforms or if they were playing in uniforms for the first time. It is not known if Old Capitol had team uniforms or not. The game began at 3:20. In the fifth inning it was clear that the Old Capitols were taking a commanding lead. The game was called on account of darkness after the seventh inning. The final score was Old Capitol, 59, and Oconee, 32.

A supper was provided for the Oconee team by the Old Capitols. After the feast, the Old Capitols escorted the Oconees to the depot where the Eatonton team "took the cars" home. Clearly a good time was had by all.

Baseball, in the early days, must have been quite something to watch as well as to play. Other than some newspaper accounts, I don't believe that any remnants from the games exist. It would be interesting for a museum to have a uniform, ball, bat or photographs from these games. Maybe someone will uncover more information or relics of the national sport as it was played in Milledgeville.

Milledgeville's First Velocipede

S ometimes when I'm downtown I try to visualize what it looked like 150 or more years ago. In my mind's eye I can see the dirt streets with the little clouds of red dust kicked up by the feet of pedestrians, horses and mules on a hot July day in 1819. The buildings are all wood. The sidewalk is made of boards. The air hangs heavily. I stand on the corner of Hancock and Wayne under a tree, with other loafers of the day, watching the slow progress of a few wagons heading toward the new prison located on the square where Georgia College & State University would be in the twentieth century.

All of a sudden, my eye is attracted by a strange contraption crossing Wilkinson Street. What in the world is that? It's a Velocipede, I'm told. It's the first one to make an appearance in Milledgeville.

I head down the street to get a closer look. The newspaper, the *Georgia Journal*, carried a long article on the Velocipede in 1819. It is entirely made of wood except for the padded seat. Seventy-five years later it would be best described as a bicycle without pedals. But in 1819, there were no bicycles and nothing else like it. The machine caused quite a stir.

To operate or ride it, one sits on the seat with feet in contact with the ground. Most of the weight of the rider rests on the Velocipede. The front wheel is turned by a rudder rather than by bicycle handlebars. The feet propel the machine forward as the rider strides forward taking long steps with feet lightly on the ground. It is recommended that the strides be taken slowly to allow the machine to cover ground between steps. One must practice to get the feel for the machine as there is danger of the rear wheel coming in contact with the heel of the foot. The rider is cautioned "only after having acquired dexterity in the equilibrium and direction of the Velocipede, that the attempt to increase the motion of the feet, or to keep them elevated while it is in rapid motion, ought to be attempted."

However, once the machine is mastered, its performance is quite impressive. It is claimed that uphill it can travel as fast as a man can walk. On the flat it will go six or seven miles per hour, which in 1819 was fast. If the road is flat, dry and firm, a speed of eight or nine miles per hour is claimed. That is the speed of a galloping horse. It is said that on the downhill, the Velocipede can reach speeds equaling, or exceeding, the skill and courage of the rider. Accidents would occur, too, sometimes with spectacular results.

With wooden wheels, no springs on the seat, rough roads and no brakes, the Velocipede is a challenge to ride safely and comfortably at normal speeds, let alone downhill. It is easy to visualize the rider bouncing over ruts while frantically attempting to stop by dragging his feet.

Unfortunately, the rider of the first Velocipede in Milledgeville is not named in the newspaper. This unsung adventurer would have created quite a stir in town. I like to think that out in the country this traveler, striding along on his Velocipede, would have created even more of a spectacle. Imagine what fascinating tracks he would have left behind. The thin overlapping track we recognize as being left by a bicycle would have been unknown at that time. To further complicate the track would be the very widely spaced footprints of the rider as he long-stepped his way toward the horizon and into history.

MILLEDGEVILLE'S
FIRST MUSEUM

Today we take museums for granted. They are numerous and often specialized in their collections. Today's museums are open to the public and are either free or charge a nominal entry fee. This was not always the case.

The traditional European museum of the eighteenth century restricted use to scholars and aristocrats. This exclusiveness went along with restrictions on the spread of knowledge and education to the public.

Education and the spread of knowledge was looked upon differently in the American colonies and in the young republic after the American Revolution. The first museum on this continent, the Charleston Museum in Charleston, South Carolina, was opened in 1773 and is still in existence. All people were encouraged to see the exhibits and develop their own thoughts and values from this new source of knowledge.

In 1786, the famous artist, inventor, educator and natural historian, Charles Willson Peale, established the first public museum in Philadelphia. He later opened branches in Baltimore and New York. The New American Museum opened in New York in 1810.

Milledgeville was not far behind the cutting edge in the museum field. In 1817, the clerk of the Baldwin Inferior Court, Abner Locke, opened a museum here. His "small collection of Antiquities & Curiosities" was located in the home of George W. King on West Greene Street. Mr. Locke "earnestly solicited the patriotic aid of his fellow citizens in collecting and preserving the Antiquities and Curiosities of his country."

Two and a half years later, Abner Locke's museum was located on the corner of Wayne and McIntosh. He described his museum "room" as containing "a variety of American Antiquities, portraits, paintings, landscapes, etc, and is attended by a portrait and miniature painter lately from New York, who is furnished with a complete collection of materials for carrying on business to the satisfaction of employers, and exhibits of his performance, etc." Locke also provided "music on the organ and violin, by Master Jacob Skinner." Admission was twenty-five cents. He continued to solicit donations from the public.

The Milledgeville public did not let him down. In 1819, Mr. Locke listed the names of over 150 persons who had made donations. I would suggest this may be a larger percentage of the adult population of Milledgeville than supports similar projects today. I noticed several Revolutionary War veterans and prominent names from the early history of Milledgeville in the list. I cannot help but wonder what items these people contributed and what may have become of those items.

I am unaware of any mention of Abner Locke or his museum after October 1820. He may have died, moved, closed or sold his museum. At that time his museum was located in "his building, east of the courthouse, a few steps north of the Planters Hotel."

Even if his museum did not survive, he was in the forefront of the American museum tradition. He, and people like him, brought us the concept of a museum experience that was open to all. His was a place where people could expand their knowledge and develop their own thoughts; this concept lives on in our present museums.

CAUSE OF DEATH:
TEETHING!

TEETHING, THE NATURAL CUTTING OF a baby's new teeth, does not seem like something likely to cause death. However, between 1869 and 1904, sixty-one young Milledgeville children died and were buried in Memory Hill Cemetery with an official cause of death listed as teething. This amounts to 2.5 percent of all deaths and 18.5 percent of the deaths of children between one and two years of age.

When a teething infant died, teething was often listed as the cause when the death was actually caused by something else. However, the teething child was sometimes the victim of a well-meaning doctor who, in an attempt to "cure" teething, would administer treatment that would bring on the death of the child.

This treatment would be in the form of medications including calomel (a mercurial), opiates or a solution in which lead acetate was the principal ingredient. Also included in the treatment was the slicing of the infant's gums over an erupting tooth with the idea of allowing the tooth to break free. This was usually done with a special little lancet known as a "gum lancet." Gum slicing was thought to have the added therapeutic benefit of bleeding. Sometimes leeches were applied to the gums for the same purpose.

A teething child who was sick with cold, coughing, fever, diarrhea, vomiting, bronchitis and a variety of other diseases was often subjected to the treatments for teething. It was thought that teething was the cause of the other disorders. Dehydration was a likely cause of many of these deaths; at that time, fluid intake was not recognized as of importance. Purgatives and emetics were used even when the little patient was already suffering from diarrhea and vomiting.

Of the Milledgeville physicians in 1859, Dr. Samuel G. White would lance the gums of an infant in an attempt to resolve unrelated medical conditions. The other physicians may have taken a similar view. Throughout the late nineteenth century, the medical profession debated the value of lancing gums and the issue of whether teething was a natural process or one that actually caused other medical conditions.

The medical profession found itself going in two directions. One theory was that teething caused potentially serious medical conditions and should be actively treated. The opposite view arose when an infant was suffering serious medical problems, which were ignored and explained away as "it's just teething." It took a third view, that the symptoms were unrelated to teething and should be treated as such, before real progress was made. It was well into the twentieth century before the medical profession universally turned its back on teething as being connected to serious medical problems.

THE SPECTACULAR SUNSETS

OF 1883

S TARTING IN LATE SEPTEMBER 1883, THE sunsets in central Georgia were incredibly spectacular. Just as the sun would dip below the horizon, the sky would glow with a variety of reds in long bands with a deep blue-black star-filled sky between the bands. It was a sight that was never to be forgotten. People would stand in the streets and wonder at the display.

A few weeks after the spectacular sunsets in Milledgeville, New York City experienced "an altogether unusual and mysterious sunset." The sky became "a vivid crimson which became more and more fiery until the sky looked as though it were ablaze with the reflection of a great fire." Hundreds of people stood watching what they assumed was the reflection from a huge fire. In Poughkeepsie, up the Hudson River from New York, the fire department was called out, but the "fire" was not to be found.

In Milledgeville, the sky was described by a witness as "one of the most gorgeous heavenly displays we ever saw. The very edge of the Eastern horizon was bathed in an ocean of crimson clouds."

Some thought the cosmic light show was the "Southern Lights" or aurora australis. Keen observers, however, noticed that the colors in the sky would appear just before dawn and again just after sunset. The main body of the colors was also near the path of the sun. With the auroras, the lights would be anywhere in the sky, which was not the case with the present display.

No one in Milledgeville and, in fact, no one living in that age actually figured out what was causing the sky to show such color. It never had done so before. What had happened? The answer lay half a world away in Indonesia. On August 26, 1883, the island volcano of Krakatoa had blown up. It was one of the most devastating explosions in the history of the planet. The noise from the explosion was heard three thousand miles away. Eleven cubic miles of dust and ash was blown fifty miles into the upper atmosphere. This dust cloud spread over the entire earth.

The light from the sun, either just before rising or just after setting, would strike these tiny particles of dust and ash high in the upper atmosphere at an angle and the reflection would appear to observers on the ground in the form of the magnificent red sky.

The spectacular sunsets continued around most of the earth throughout the winter of 1884. Unusual sunsets would be common for almost three years. This veil of dust did more than just create memorable sunsets, however. It also reduced the amount of solar radiation reaching the surface of the earth. This caused a lowering of the average temperature all over the world.

In Milledgeville, January 5 would be remembered as the night that water froze one half inch thick in basins in rooms that had been warmed by a fire during the day. The temperature reached eight degrees. Kerosene froze in lamps while shivering occupants tried to keep warm. Fishing Creek was almost entirely frozen over.

While we know that the sunsets were effected by a volcano on the other side of the earth, reporters at the time did not. They looked at the phenomenon differently. The *Atlanta Journal-Constitution* commented that the brightly illuminated sunsets "caused men to drop the cares of the dead day to talk of this new, strange beauty far above them. They have lifted the thoughts of humanity at least as high as the material heavens that arch over us, if not beyond them to the power that appoints the courses of the stars." The unknowing observers of 1883 appreciated the sight far more than we who now know the cause.

ANIMALS ON THE STREETS

O NE OF THE CHARMS OF Milledgeville is that it does not take a great deal of imagination to visualize what the town looked like in the past. Substitute dirt roads, some buildings and add more open space between buildings and the mental picture begins to appear. The Milledgeville of our past also had farm animals owned by residents downtown. From the earliest days, these animals were a problem for the city.

In 1810, an ordinance for removing swine from Milledgeville had been ignored by the citizens. The board of commissioners then got tough. The town marshal was ordered to round up offending swine within the city.

Apparently, this was not effective or was ignored by the marshal as well as the citizenry. In 1883, it was again ordered by the city "that hogs shall not be allowed to run at large on the public streets within the corporate limits of the city." As an aside it was also mentioned that an ordinance was passed "prohibiting butcher's stands, and any unnecessary boxes, barrels, on the streets." The mental picture of Milledgeville becomes clearer as we add butcher stands and the obstinate hogs running at large on the streets.

In addition, there was a problem with horses and cows. In 1869, the city marshal was instructed to "see that horses are not hitched so near the side walks that they can cover the walks with their heels, to the annoyance and danger of passers by. Sidewalks are rendered unpleasant by the manure dropped." The instructions to the city marshal went on to include that "ladies very justly complain of…the droppings of cows standing or sleeping before the stable gates or milk yard." For emphasis it was mentioned that such occurrences were "common all over the city." Further, the city marshal was to "compel the owners of cows to see that their side walks are cleared off every morning the first thing, and in the evening when the cows come up, put them in the yard or stable, and not have the side walks manured as if for turnip patch purposes."

Regrettably the problem with the animals in the streets was not corrected, perhaps not even improved. In 1890, the city once again passed an ordinance stating as of February 1, "it shall be unlawful for cattle and geese to run at large in this city." Offending cattle and geese were to be rounded up and impounded by the city. The owners had ninety-six hours to pay the fines or the animals would be sold.

Fines included the amount of board for each animal while in custody, and two dollars per capita for all cattle and twenty-five cents for all geese. The city officer who rounded up the animals was to receive one dollar for each "herd of cattle" and twenty-five cents for each goose.

The mental picture of Old Milledgeville now includes city officers rounding up "herds" of cattle, as well as chasing down geese, on the streets. The activities of the city marshal must have been a topic of conversation for the street loafers as they kept an eye on the activities of the downtown.

One might think that with the hogs, cattle and geese rounded up as well as the horses being kept off the sidewalk, everyone in Milledgeville would be pleased. This was not the case. A person known only as "Jefferson Street" wrote the newspaper with the following comment:

To the Honorable City Council of Milledgeville, allow me, a tax payer, to suggest, kindly, to your honorable body, that as the cows and geese were ordered by you to be kept up and not to run at large, the result of which action has caused the weeds and grass to grow up so that some of our streets look like a wilderness and the hands employed by your body cannot keep them clean; will you not request the citizens to turn out their cows for the month of August, as street cleaners, as it will be a benefit and blessing to all concerned.

Cows keeping the streets of Milledgeville from looking like a wilderness by being street cleaners! What a wonderful addition to the mental picture of Milledgeville this makes.

ECHOES OF LAFAYETTE'S VISIT
TO MILLEDGEVILLE

IN OCTOBER 2000, MILLEDGEVILLE CELEBRATED the 175th anniversary of the Marquis de Lafayette's 1825 visit to Milledgeville. There was a large event at the Georgia Military College campus with General Lafayette "himself" present. There were other, smaller activities in town that attracted quite a few visitors as well. While the memory of the celebration has probably faded for most, I am frequently reminded of that day.

As a member of the Friends of Baldwin County Cemeteries and owner of a musket and what, in a pinch, passes as a Revolutionary War militiaman's attire, I was somehow talked into making an appearance at Memory Hill Cemetery. Members of the Friends were stationed at various points of interest in the cemetery with the idea of talking with visitors. My duties were to stand at the grave of Revolutionary War veteran Samuel Beckham and regale visitors with whatever knowledge I possessed of Samuel Beckham, the Revolutionary War, Memory Hill, my odd outfit and anything else the moment required. My repertoire on Samuel Beckham was rather short: he was a captain in the militia during the Revolutionary War and later was a major stationed at Fort Wilkinson, just South of Milledgeville.

The day was hot. We had a great turnout in the cemetery with many visitors. It sccmcd as if I was talking with interested people for hours. At one point I had just finished talking with a small group and turned to step back into the shade. As I turned, I found myself face to face with a man carrying a musket and dressed as I was. Faced with this apparition I quickly stuck out my hand and said, "Welcome to Memory Hill." It later occurred to me that might have been his line. My Revolutionary War visitor shook my hand and introduced himself as Mickey Beckham. To say I was startled is an understatement. I confess to an uneasy glance at the gravestone of Samuel Beckham and wondering if I might have been out in the sun too long or if maybe something really strange was going on.

Mickey, who lives in South Carolina, explained to me that he had heard about Milledgeville's Lafayette celebration and that his Beckham relative, Samuel, would be featured in Memory Hill. So he had borrowed the musket and Revolutionary War clothing so he could attend in grand style. He was not a ghost. We talked history for a long time. He helped me out with visitors who would now hear about Samuel Beckham straight from the mouth of a Beckham. He was a great success.

Mickey and I exchanged email addresses and I thought I'd probably never hear from him again. How wrong I was. Little did I know but while in Memory Hill Cemetery, Mickey had been bitten by the Revolutionary War history bug. He has been consumed by an infection for which there is no cure.

He returned to South Carolina fired up to learn about the Revolutionary War in his area of the Upcountry. To his surprise and delight, he discovered that there was a little-known battle, or skirmish, in 1780 at a wide spot in the road in the area known today as Beckhamville, near Great Falls. He researched this engagement and discovered it not only has real historical significance but has been overlooked by the public as well as historians.

Mickey set about to correct the problem. He established the Beckhamville Battlefield Society whose goal is to promote a greater understanding among the public of the Revolutionary War in South Carolina. In 2002, the first annual Battle of Beckhamville reenactment took place. It was a great success. In 2003, the event drew even more people and received newspaper coverage over a wide area. The reenactments include not just the battle but also an encampment of reenactors who give demonstrations of soldier and civilian life in the 1780s. It is great fun with a lot to learn for the visitor.

Mickey can't get enough of the Revolutionary War. Besides going to the reenactments of other battles, he is in the process of writing a novel about the Revolutionary War in South Carolina. His own family, including our Samuel Beckham, appear in the novel. Mickey continually researches details for his book. He confidently interviews doctors, lawyers and historians and not only learns about the war but learns the details of life in Revolutionary South Carolina. He has acquired a knowledge of the past that would astonish his friends.

Mickey and I maintain contact by email, phone and occasional visits. I attend his battle reenactments and even once found myself standing in a field and firing a few shots with my musket before being killed by the enemy. Occasionally, Mickey will ask my opinion about some historical detail that he is including in his novel. I do my best to help him but he's way ahead of me and running fast. We talk a lot of history, exchange ideas and generally have a great time with the Revolutionary War.

Mickey traces his newfound passion for the Revolutionary War to meeting me at Memory Hill Cemetery. However, I'm not taking the blame for his obsession, I'm laying the responsibility right where it belongs: with the Marquis de Lafayette.

JETT THOMAS'S UNIQUE
DYING PROPOSITION

JETT THOMAS WAS ONE OF Milledgeville's early residents. He is remembered for many achievements in his life, but not for one of the most unusual propositions ever advanced by a dying man.

Jett Thomas was born in May 1776 in Culpepper County, Virginia. As a child he migrated with his family to Georgia. He was a carpenter by trade. Later he became a building contractor. He, along with John B. Scott, built the State House in Milledgeville. He also built a two-story building on the northeast corner of Elbert and Franklin Streets where he ran a tavern and inn described as a "house of entertainment."

In 1802, he was a justice of the peace for Clarke County. He also represented Clarke County in the Georgia House of Representatives from 1805 to 1807. He built one of the first buildings of what would become the University of Georgia.

During the War of 1812, Jett Thomas was captain of the Baldwin Volunteer Artillery from Milledgeville. He was under the command of General John Floyd in the campaign against the Creeks known as the Creek War. Jett Thomas and his artillery saw action in what is now Alabama, at the battle of Autosee in November of 1813. In a desperate struggle, in January 1814 at the nighttime battle of Calabee Creek, Jett Thomas's artillery was firing at the enemy only yards away.

When their enlistment was up, Jett Thomas brought his men back to Milledgeville. He remained in the service and was promoted to major. Later he would be promoted to colonel. After the war, in November 1816, he was elected by the Georgia legislature to the position of major general commanding the Third Division of the Georgia militia.

By this time Jett Thomas was a very sick man. He had cancer of the mouth. He consulted local doctors and traveled to consult with other doctors but could not find a cure.

In late 1816 and the first two weeks of 1817, this statement appeared in newspapers all over the South:

General Thomas, of Milledgeville, has requested the Editors of the Georgia Journal, to make known, that he will give two thousand dollars, and pay all requisite expenses, to any person who will cure him of a cancer in his mouth. Printers throughout the Union by diffusing this invitation, may perhaps prolong the life of a valuable citizen.

In 1817, $2,000 was equal in value to about $22,500 in today's dollars. Clearly, as his life was on the line, Jett Thomas was withholding nothing as he had nothing to lose and everything to gain if successful. Unfortunately, Jett Thomas died January 6, 1817, at the age of forty, while newspapers continued to print appeals for his cure. A funeral procession consisting of clergymen, physicians, chief mourners, military and citizens wound its way through Milledgeville to pay their last respects to General Jett Thomas. He was buried with full military honors.

Putting out such an "invitation," or proposition, in newspapers in an effort to find a medical cure for a disease is certainly unusual. Some might say that it is unique to Jett Thomas. The only other case I am aware of took place eighty years later and coincidentally also involved a person from Milledgeville. Dixie Haygood, perhaps better known as "the Little Georgia Magnet, Annie Abbott," advertised for someone to cure her of her "powers," which she claimed was causing severe headaches. Her appeal appeared to be a use of the press to hype her own career. Jett Thomas was sincere in his proposal.

A weathered tombstone stands over Jett Thomas's grave in Memory Hill. As it is difficult to read, visitors usually pass by and the grave is forgotten. The man whose grave it marks, however, should not be forgotten, as he did a great deal in his life. He also left a dying proposition that after almost two hundred years is still unique.

MAD DOG!

T HOUGH VERY RARE NOW, THE cry of "Mad dog! Mad dog!" would strike fear in the hearts of pedestrians. A rabid, or "mad" dog, would bite other animals and people without any provocation. The animal would go on biting until it was killed.

In Milledgeville, the cry of "Mad dog!" would immediately result in an armed gang of men following the sick animal through town and firing shots at it. Before 1900, this scene, unfortunately, was a relatively common occurrence. There was no other way to deal with a rabid animal than to kill it as soon as possible.

The bite from a rabid dog would almost always produce death. It was an agonizing death, and the patient might linger for several days or more than a week in constant torment. There was no effective treatment for rabies, or hydrophobia as it was improperly called.

Despite there being no treatment, those bitten or their loved ones would seek out what was considered a remedy: the madstone. The madstone is a hairball obtained from the stomach of an animal. In some cases it is composed of the matted hair which the animal has licked from its body or masses of vegetable fibers which have formed over a long period of time into a ball in its stomach.

The procedure was to apply the madstone to the bite wound. It was believed that the longer the madstone stuck to the wound, the higher the probability of it preventing rabies. We know today that the length of time the madstone would stick depended upon the amount of blood flowing from the wound. The more blood, the more adhesive the effect, as it would coagulate into the porous madstone.

Madstones gained an individual reputation. Some were considered better than others depending on how successful they had been in "preventing" rabies. These legendary madstones were eagerly sought after by those desperate souls who had been bitten or were trying to procure a madstone for a friend or relative. Large sums of money would transfer for the loan of a "good" madstone. The madstones themselves would be handed down in a family through generations. A particularly "good" stone would even acquire a name such as "the Bezoar stone of the East Indies."

In January of 1897, Benjamin W. Hunt of Eatonton, Georgia, was bitten by a cat. A couple of days later the cat died. Hunt, suspecting that the cat may have been rabid, knew his life was in jeopardy. Hunt was a wealthy dairyman and banker and had the means as well as the scientific education to understand that if the cat was rabid he had only one real chance for successful treatment. He immediately took the train to New York, bringing the body of the cat with him. He consulted with the chief physician of the Pasteur Institute and turned over the cat for examination. As the results of the autopsy of the cat would take two weeks and the incubation period of rabies was two weeks to two months, Hunt decided that he would travel on to Paris, France, to put himself under the care of Dr. Louis Pasteur himself.

Hunt left New York the following morning on a ship sailing for France. He spent several weeks taking the treatment at the Pasteur Institute, then returned home to Eatonton. In the process he became convinced that Georgia needed such a medical facility.

Through the efforts of Benjamin Hunt, the Pasteur Institute in Atlanta was formed in 1900. Georgians could now be treated for rabies by a proven, successful method. No longer would people need to rely on useless madstones for a cure. The death rate at the Pasteur Institute was about 1 percent. In 1908, the Pasteur Institute was taken over by the Georgia health department.

As for the madstones, they are still with us. As incredible as it sounds, there are still people who seek treatment for rabies with madstones. As the vast majority of dogs now get rabies vaccinations, the incidence of rabies is very rare and the use of madstones or the effective Pasteur method are seldom required.

THE DRAMATIC END TO THE LIFE OF HENRY BYROM, GAMBLER

A T MIDNIGHT, ONE NOVEMBER EVENING in 1833, the life of a locally notorious gambler came to an end in a hail of gunfire.

Henry Byrom, a well-educated young man from Hancock County, had been set up by his family as a merchant. Unfortunately, he became infatuated with gambling. One evening, after drinking and gambling heavily, he found he had lost a large sum of money and was deeply in debt to the gambling establishment. He returned the following night determined to recover his losses or lose everything in the attempt.

By the end of the evening, Byrom had lost not only all his money, but his store and all its stock of goods. He was ruined. Allegedly, Byrom swore an oath that he would learn the "devilish arts" of the gambler and would make his living by preying on his fellow man. He admitted that he was no longer a respectable citizen. He became one of the more expert of the "sporting men" in Georgia. He played for high stakes, drank heavily and was considered a gentlemanly desperado.

In 1832, on the streets of Macon, Byrom bullied a man into an informal duel. It was just before dawn, when they met on the street after several days of insults. In what would be recognized 150 years later as a grade-B Western movie, Byrom was seen backing down the street holding his hands out calling to passersby to notice that he was being threatened at gun point. The bullied and now enraged gunman slowly approached Byrom with a pistol in his hand.

Byrom drew his own pistol and fired. Thomas M. Ellis fell, his pistol discharging harmlessly as his arm hit the ground. Byrom calmly sought out witnesses to testify that he had acted in self defense. Ellis died but Byrom was acquitted.

In the early evening a year later, in Milledgeville, one of Byrom's friends, a Colonel Ward, was shot by Robert McComb during an altercation at McComb's tavern on Wayne Street. Byrom loudly proclaimed that McComb was responsible. Byrom raged that McComb and all who backed him (which was a considerable number, as the consensus was McComb had acted in self defense), were cowards. Byrom dared them to "fight it out" with him. He took out his watch and declared, "I appoint twelve o'clock this night to die, and invite you all to my funeral."

McComb, along with his supporters, had armed themselves and taken refuge in the upstairs of the building. Byrom walked back and forth at the bottom of the stairs raving to the watching crowd that he would get revenge. At midnight he exclaimed, "Come, it is time!" and, armed with pistols and a sword, began to charge up the stairs. Before reaching the second step, he was met with a "volley of musketry" and died instantly.

Dead at twenty-seven, Henry Byrom the gambler was carried in a funeral procession to Memory Hill the following day. His casket was accompanied by a large number of friends, fellow citizens and many members of the legislature which was then in session.

His obituary mentioned his "unexpected demise" and that the funeral service was performed "with a solemnity suited to the occasion." It was also mentioned that Byrom "possessed all those high, honorable, and perhaps too sensitive feelings, which mark the Southern character. He was the victim of an acute sensibility, which honor and honesty [are] too often sacrificed at their own hallowed shrine."

A week after the funeral, Byrom's mother had his remains disinterred and reburied in a family cemetery in Hancock County. Today the location of his grave is unknown. Colonel Ward, whose gunshot wound precipitated the actions of Byrom, survived his wound. Robert McComb continued to lead a respectable life in Milledgeville.

We often hear that long ago Milledgeville was a pretty wild place, particularly when the legislature was in session. The lifestyle and death of Henry Byrom, the gambler, help illustrate the point.

OLD JIM

IN 1843, AN OLD MAN DIED in Milledgeville. He is known to us only as Jim. Jim had been a slave of James Thomas during the Revolutionary War and was his personal servant. After the Revolution, James Thomas came to Georgia and brought Jim with him.

Veterans of the American Revolution were few when Jim died in 1843. They were old men who fought in a war that had ended sixty years ago. Jim, however, was not just a veteran of the American Revolution. He was also a veteran of the French and Indian War. He had been at Braddock's Defeat, July 9, 1755, eighty-eight years earlier. He was said to be 112 years of age at his death, which would give him a birth year of 1731.

Oddly, Jim and those around him lived to incredible, perhaps unbelievable, ages. His former master, James Thomas, died at the age of 80, which was considered very old at that time. Martha, James Thomas's wife, was born in 1747 and died in Milledgeville in 1857 at the age of 109.

Jim left a widow, Fanny. Fanny's age is not known. However, it was said that her youngest daughter was a "grown woman at the time the British had possession of Savannah." Savannah fell to the British in 1778. If this daughter was 18 at that time, then she would have been born in 1760. As she was Fanny's "youngest daughter", Fanny herself must have been born no later than 1740. At the time of Jim's death, Fanny would have been about 103, at least. It is unknown when she died. The most long-lived of them all, however, is Fanny's mother. It is said that she died in 1808, at the age of 120.

In 1844, a tombstone was erected on Jim's grave. Regrettably, his marker is no longer visible. Martha Thomas's gravestone was visible in 1939 but it, too, no longer exists. The Revolutionary War veteran James Thomas's original tombstone is gone but it has been replaced by a Veterans Administration marker probably dating from the 1930s.

In this family's household, it appears their gravestones don't last as long as the people they memorialized. Flesh may indeed be stronger than stone.

THE PRESIDENTIAL CANDIDATE
FROM MILLEDGEVILLE

JIMMY CARTER WAS THE FIRST U.S. president from Georgia. There was another Georgian who ran for president. I'm referring to Milledgeville's William Gibbs McAdoo.

McAdoo was born near Marietta on October 31, 1863. Shortly thereafter, in an effort to avoid the violence of the Civil War, the family fled to Milledgeville. McAdoo's father, William G. McAdoo Sr., was a lawyer and practiced in Milledgeville until 1878, when he accepted the position as a professor at the University of Tennessee.

McAdoo lived in Midway and Milledgeville until about fifteen years of age. He then went to the University of Tennessee for a short time before being appointed deputy clerk of the United States Circuit Court for the Southern Division, Eastern District of Tennessee in 1882. After studying law, he was admitted to the bar in 1885. After practicing law for several years in Tennessee, he moved to New York City.

He flourished in New York. He became president of the Hudson and Manhattan Railroad Company. This company built and operated the first railroad tunnels under the Hudson River between New York City and New Jersey. Those tunnels were known as the McAdoo tubes.

In 1912, as president of the Democratic National Committee, McAdoo promoted Woodrow Wilson in his bid for the presidency. After Wilson was elected, McAdoo was appointed to the position of secretary of the treasury. He married President Wilson's daughter, Eleanor, in a White House ceremony in 1914.

He was a contender for the Democratic nomination in 1920. He ran again in 1924 and came very close to being selected as the nominee. His main opponent for the nomination was Alfred E. Smith, the governor of New York.

Milledgeville was strongly supportive of McAdoo. A Baldwin County Women's McAdoo Club was formed in February 1924. Among the members were Mrs. C.P. Crawford, Mrs. H.D. Allen, Mrs. R.B. Moore and Mrs. Charles Moore. The ladies made plans to promote "our native son for President."

At that time, the Democratic party required that the nominee get two thirds of the votes to win the nomination. The convention was stalemated between Al Smith and McAdoo.

On the 103ʳᵈ ballot the Democrats agreed to drop both Smith and McAdoo in favor of John W. Davis as a compromise candidate.

The election was a landslide for the Republican candidate, Calvin Coolidge, who received 382 electoral votes to the Democrat's 136. McAdoo wasn't through with politics, however. From 1933 to 1938, he was a U.S. senator from California.

McAdoo didn't forget about Milledgeville, or cut all ties, after he left. He returned once in the 1890s and again in 1918 and 1923. In 1918, he was secretary of the treasury and director general of the railroads. He came to Milledgeville in a private railroad car on a special train. McAdoo was met at the station by prominent citizens who had been his boyhood friends. He went to the Georgia Normal and Industrial College where he gave a talk to the young ladies. Later he visited Georgia Military College where he also spoke.

He was given a tour of the town and also of Midway where he lived in his earliest years. He also toured the house on South Jefferson, which still stands, where he lived after moving from Midway in the late 1860s.

In 1923, the visit was almost a repeat of the 1918 visit. This time he spoke at Georgia State College for Women, where he urged the ladies to vote. He also toured Allen's Home, the private sanitarium where ninety-six shell shocked World War I veterans were being treated. He again visited his old homes in Midway and Milledgeville and places where he played as a boy.

At the time of his death, he was chairman of the board of a steamship company in California. He died on a trip to Washington, D.C., in 1941 and is buried in Arlington National Cemetery.

Hillsborough — Baldwin County's First Courthouse

W HEN WE LOOK AT OUR modern courthouse, we are not reminded of our past. Across the street is the "Old Courthouse," which is only about 120 years old. It roughly occupies the location of some of the previous courthouses. The first courthouse in Baldwin County, however, was not situated there. In fact, it wasn't even in Milledgeville.

The first courthouse was located in what is now Putnam County. The boundaries of Baldwin County have been changed many times. In 1805, Baldwin County included parts of what are now Jones, Putnam, Jasper and Morgan Counties.

The county seat was at a place called Hillsborough, six miles east of what is now Eatonton on the road to Sparta, on state Route 16. Hillsborough wasn't a metropolis. It consisted of a few crude homes and a couple of stores and grogshops, some of which were owned by the Hill family. The location is easy to find today. As one travels east from Eatonton, Pea Ridge Road is passed on the right on a downhill slope. At the bottom of this hill is Crooked Creek. Hillsborough was located on the eastern side of Crooked Creek at the intersection with what is now called Old Phoenix Road. Back in the undergrowth, about seventy-five feet, on the northwest corner of Route 16 and Old Phoenix Road, is an old millstone. In the 1930s, this millstone was used to display a bronze plaque, now stolen, which marked the site of the early courthouse. Fortunately, the millstone has proved too inconvenient for thieves to remove.

In 1806, the first election of local officials for Baldwin County took place in the log home of George Hill. Mr. Hill's home was used as Baldwin County's first courthouse. The superior court met there in 1807.

As far as I know, only two significant events occurred in Hillsborough. A couple of men were tried and convicted of murder. They were hanged and buried there. As recently as the 1870s, their graves were still visible. I have not been able to locate the graves; they probably have now vanished.

The other noteworthy occurrence was that my great, great, great grandparents, James Zachry and Polly Flournoy, obtained their marriage license there in May of 1807.

In the fall of 1807, the court was transferred to Milledgeville where the first court session was held in January of 1808 in the State House. Putnam County was carved out of Baldwin County. For two years, Hillsborough was the county seat of Putnam County before being transferred to Eatonton.

Hillsborough was finished. After a while, the Hills and the other residents drifted on. Their buildings decayed and disappeared. The chimney of George Hill's house was still standing in the 1860s, a lone reminder of the first courthouse of Baldwin County, but it too has been long gone. All that's left is the unmarked millstone, now buried in vegetation.

THE GREAT ROOSTER
RIP-OFF OF 1903

H ISTORY IS THE KNOWLEDGE OF past events and especially those of human affairs. Usually we speak about soldiers, statesmen, murders or murderers. We also have discussed horrific natural occurrences such as tornadoes and volcanic eruptions. Sometimes we speak of sports figures or buildings or events. Most of these topics can claim at least some prominence or fame.

But history isn't always about earthshaking events. It also concerns everyday events, and people of the past. One event that had no lasting consequences, except perhaps that it is being mentioned here over a hundred years after it occurred, I call the Great Rooster Rip-Off of 1903.

The story takes place in the fall of 1903. The editor of one of Milledgeville's local newspapers was eager to increase interest in and the circulation of his paper. He decided upon the idea of having a contest. Many people always are eager to participate in contests with the hope of winning some sort of prize. Others watch from the sidelines in breathless anticipation.

The editor came up with a clever idea. He obtained a Plymouth Rock Rooster that he exhibited outside the newspaper office. Subscribers to the paper were encouraged to determine the number of feathers on this particular rooster and send in their best guess. The person with the guess closest to the actual number of feathers would win.

The contest was to end on a specified day. The rooster was to be killed and a panel of competent experts was to sit down with the remains, pluck the feathers and count them. The experts, and the factors involved in determining who would be chosen to sit on the esteemed panel, are unknown.

A huge interest in the proceedings was generated. Sales of the newspaper were booming. Guesses were pouring in to the newspaper office. The enterprising editor was delighted. All his plans were going perfectly.

Then, the unthinkable happened. As usual, the editor went to his office very early in the morning, as editors are wont to do, and discovered that a crime had been committed.

The rooster was standing in his cage staring at the editor with little beady eyes and a very quizzical look, but sporting only a few feathers. Some Milledgeville miscreant had come in the dark of night and plucked the rooster of nearly all his feathers and taken the feathers away.

The bird was put on display by the angry editor. Hundreds of disappointed contestants and other citizens came to gawk at the spectacle. Rumors and accusations flew in all directions, but the villain was never apprehended. The best efforts of the local constabulary turned up no clues. No one ever confessed. The criminal did not crow of the accomplishment but took his, or her, guilty secret to the grave.

The Ladies' Artillery Company
of Jefferson Street

During the summer of 1875, it was announced in the *Union Recorder* that "the ladies on Jefferson Street have organized an artillery company."

Unfortunately, that is all the firm information available. Research has been unable to determine who these women were, why they organized an artillery company or what has become of the company, let alone their artillery.

Some may think that the formation of such a company is preposterous. However, it has happened before in other places. In 1900, a group of young ladies in New Brunswick formed Company A, Sixty-Second St. John Fusilliers. They were an infantry company and volunteered to go to China to fight in the Boxer Rebellion.

In 1775, during the crisis of the Lexington/Concord battles, the women of the town of Pepperell, Massachusetts, were left alone when their men answered the call to fight the British. The ladies immediately formed their own militia company, complete with officers and sergeants, to defend their town. They donned their husbands' trousers and shirts and armed themselves with everything from muskets to pitchforks. They patrolled the streets and guarded the bridges. A couple of Tories, apparently carrying dispatches for the British, were captured by the company and held until they could be turned over to proper authorities. These women continued under arms and maintained law and order until their men returned.

During the Revolutionary War, many women are thought to have provided assistance to the gun crews. Fighting in the infantry was problematic for a woman, but it didn't take a man to carry powder, shot or handle the rammer or sponge. Artillery actually is a military art that women can physically handle better than many other military activities.

The lack of information on the ladies of Jefferson Street and their artillery does not mean the company failed. At that time there were many places in the vicinity for the ladies to drill and to fire their pieces. There is no more reason for the women's artillery company to disband than for a male unit to disband.

One cannot help but wonder at the wording of the announcement. Since it is specified that the "ladies on Jefferson street" are involved in the organization, does that mean that ladies from Wilkinson Street or some other part of town could not join them? Or, perhaps ladies other than those on Jefferson Street had their own artillery companies?

It is very tempting to determine what ladies lived on Jefferson Street in 1875 and try to deduce which of them belonged to the artillery company. I, however, have not done so.

Lastly, because research has not unearthed any indication that the ladies' artillery company ever disbanded, it has crossed my mind that perhaps it is still in existence. I will keep an open mind on the subject.

JOANNA TROUTMAN
AND THE FLAG OF TEXAS

MILLEDGEVILLE HAS MANY INTERESTING CONNECTIONS with the 1835–1836 Texas War for Independence. One of those Milledgevillians associated with Texas is Joanna Troutman.

She was born in Milledgeville in 1818 and received her early education in Scottsboro. Her Milledgeville roots were well established. Her grandfather, John Troutman, was murdered in his bed at his home on the southwest corner of Hancock and Clarke Streets in 1819. Her father, Hiram Troutman, lived in the same house when Joanna was born. After the death of Joanna's mother, Hiram Troutman married Sarah Bird Lamar, the daughter of early Milledgeville resident Thompson Bird and the widow of the superior court Justice L.Q.C. Lamar, who died in 1834.

In the fall of 1835, Joanna was living in Knoxville, in Crawford County, with her father and step-mother. Knoxville is located on highway 80 southwest of Macon. Texas, at that time, was a province of Mexico. There were many Americans living there and they were clamoring for independence from Mexico. The United States was officially neutral on the issue of Texas's independence, but many volunteers from many states headed for Texas. Jim Bowie and Davy Crockett are probably the best known of the volunteers. However, about 120 men from Georgia formed the Georgia Battalion and offered their services to the Texans. Georgia supplied these men with weapons from the arsenal in Milledgeville.

Joanna Troutman, at seventeen years old, was very interested in Texas's independence, as several of her family were involved. She got the idea to make a flag for the Georgia Battalion to take with them to Texas. She designed and made the flag herself. It was made of white silk with a five-pointed sky blue star in the center. On one side of the flag was written, "Texas and Liberty" and on the other, in Latin, "Where Liberty dwells there is my country."

When the unit was marching from Macon to Columbus, it passed through the little town of Knoxville. There, they were presented with the flag by Joanna Troutman. They carried it with them to Texas. It was unfurled over the Americana Hotel in Velasco on

January 8, 1836. Later, the Georgia Battalion joined Colonel James W. Fannin at Goliad. When Fannin heard that independence had been declared on March 2, 1836, he ordered Joanna Troutman's flag raised as the national flag.

Within the next few weeks, the Georgia Battalion was defeated in several battles, and they surrendered to the Mexicans. In an act of treachery, hundreds of American prisoners at Goliad were executed along with Fannin and his command in what has become known as Fannin's Massacre. The flag was lost.

In late April, the Texans won a major victory at San Jacinto over General Santa Anna, the Mexican leader. Among the spoils of victory was the silverware of Santa Anna. The first minister of the Republic of Texas to the United States passed through Milledgeville and gave a spoon and fork from the set to Georgia's Governor William Schley, with the request that they be sent to Joanna Troutman.

Joanna Troutman died in 1879 in Crawford County and was buried in an unmarked grave. In 1913, the State of Texas arranged for her body to be moved to the state cemetery at Austin. In 1919, a large bronze sculpture depicting Joanna Troutman was erected in the cemetery in her memory. A life-size painting of her hangs in the Texas state capitol building. The lone star of Joanna Troutman's flag is still on the flag of Texas.

THE BATTLE OF THE
BALDWIN-PUTNAM BRIDGE

A S WE DRIVE NORTH ON Route 441 from Milledgeville, we quite casually drive over the bridge by the power plant without giving it much thought. A bit more than fifty years ago, Sinclair Dam was not complete and the bridge there was much shorter. Instead of crossing an arm of Lake Sinclair, the bridge spanned what was known as Little River.

One hundred years ago things were very different. To get across Little River, one had to use a ferry. In the fall of 1903, the Baldwin County commissioners thought it would be good for business to have a bridge over Little River. They authorized the purchase of lumber and set the project in motion. Businessmen and farmers in both Putnam and Baldwin Counties were delighted.

Not everyone was pleased with the project. Immediately, two sisters, Mary and Lula Humber, heirs of R.C. Humber, had their attorneys get an injunction to have the work stopped. They claimed that they held the water rights to Little River and that no bridge could be built across it. They did not mention that the bridge was two miles downstream from their ferry, which would be forced out of business if the bridge was to open. These ladies hired several attorneys to work on the case, but the one we remember today was Carl Vinson. Carl Vinson, of course, would go on to represent the 6th District for fifty years in the U.S. House of Representatives and chair the Armed Services Committee. The aircraft carrier USS *Carl Vinson* is named for him. But, that is in the future; at this time he was just nineteen years old. Things looked good for the Humber sisters as the judge ruled in their favor, saying that the county had improperly handled the bridge transaction.

The Baldwin County commissioners could not build the bridge. So they sold the lumber to private individuals. While the Humbers and their lawyers were quietly savoring their victory, work continued furiously on the bridge. Those who knew it was being built kept quiet. In just a few days the bridge was completed and was being used.

Within hours of the completion of the bridge, word was spreading through Milledgeville that the bridge was open to traffic. The Humber sisters and their lawyers were completely taken by surprise. They decided to take direct action in response.

The sisters and their lawyers, Carl Vinson and Edward R. Hines, went to the bridge. What did they do? They got out their axes and started chopping out the center section. The two ladies worked along with the men tearing out planks and cutting pilings. They cut out the entire center section and dropped it into the river. When the Humber sisters and their attorneys returned to Milledgeville, they were served with arrest warrants. Yes, Carl Vinson was arrested. They each posted bond of fifty dollars. The following night, the bridge was rebuilt by persons unknown. Traffic continued to flow across the bridge.

The legal battles continued. The Humbers asserted that their grandfather had bought the water rights in 1860. Among other things, they also claimed that a member of the grand jury, Peter J. Cline, should not be allowed on the grand jury as he was one of the instigators in the bridge building and thus would be prejudiced against them. Mr. Cline was chairman of the Board of Trade and a very prominent businessman in Milledgeville. It was clearly in his best interests, and in the interests of his business acquaintances, that the bridge be built. The judge agreed that Mr. Cline could not be on the grand jury when it considered the bridge case.

Charges were eventually dropped against the Humber sisters, Edward Hines and Carl Vinson. The superior court ruled against the Humbers. The strange case of the bridge between Putnam and Baldwin was over. But it was not to be forgotten.

For many years thereafter the bridge across Little River between Putnam and Baldwin Counties was known as Cline Bridge. I can't help but wonder how many times in the following seventy-seven years did Carl Vinson cross that bridge and think of his early case with a smile.

BENJAMIN TALBERT — REVOLUTIONARY SOLDIER

IN THE HEART OF MEMORY Hill Cemetery is the tombstone marking the grave of the Revolutionary War soldier Benjamin Talbert. Unfortunately, his name is misspelled on the tombstone as "Tolbert." Further, his service is inscribed on the stone as "Georgia Troops." It seems that those who ordered his marker from the U.S. government, probably in the 1930s, may have been so eager to mark the grave of a Revolutionary War soldier that they were a bit too hasty in their research.

Benjamin Talbert was the son of Joseph and Rebeccah Talbert and served in the Virginia Militia. He married Mary Whaley of Loudon County, Virginia, in 1780. They lived in Virginia until about 1790 and then moved to Georgia. They initially lived in Wilkes County and later moved to Baldwin.

Benjamin Talbert drew land in the 1827 land lottery. He also applied for a pension in 1833 for his service in the Revolutionary War. His pension application is available through the National Archives (#S16548) and makes interesting reading.

The application was made in Baldwin County on February 27, 1833. The sixty-eight-year-old veteran appeared before famous judge L.Q.C. Lamar of the superior court. Talbert swears that in about 1780, when he was fifteen, he volunteered at Fredericksburg, Virginia, for a tour of three months in the militia. His unit was part of the command of the Marquis de Lafayette. One cannot help but wonder the thoughts, emotions and old memories that must have gone through Talbert's mind when, in 1825, Lafayette visited Milledgeville.

Later, he was again called out as a militiaman. Talbert mentions being in an action where his unit was engaged in an attack on British General Lord Cornwallis at the James River. In his most memorable engagement, his unit was surprised by British Lieutenant Colonel Banastre Tarleton's cavalry, which attacked at dawn. The cavalrymen rode double with an infantryman behind each horseman. The foot soldiers dismounted and the cavalry charged. Talbert's officer called out to his men to save themselves and fled on horseback, abandoning his men. Tarleton had a fearsome reputation for brutality and not taking prisoners. The unit was scattered with many Patriots killed or wounded. Talbert ran into the woods, eluded capture and was able to return to his command the following day.

His tour of duty expired about the time that George Washington laid siege to Cornwallis at Yorktown. After the surrender of the British army, Talbert again served as part of a guard as British prisoners were transported to prison camps.

In 1833, Benjamin Talbert had no evidence that he had served in the Revolutionary War. His discharge papers had long since been lost. A minister, Edward Brantley, and Dr. Tomlinson Fort swore that they were well acquainted with Talbert and that he was respected and believed in this area to have been a soldier of the Revolution and that they, too, believed that Talbert was a veteran of the war. Talbert's application was approved and he received a pension for his service in a war that had been over for fifty years.

Benjamin Talbert died in 1842 or 1843. It is unknown whether he was originally buried in Memory Hill Cemetery or whether his remains were moved to the cemetery later.

DR. B.J. SIMMONS

ONE OF THE MORE INTERESTING people in Memory Hill Cemetery is buried on the south side, in a lot next to the sexton's cottage. Born in Laurens County in 1870, Benjamin Judson Simmons, through his own extraordinary efforts, educated himself. He attended Ballards Normal school in Macon and the Georgia State Industrial school at Savannah. He was a school teacher in Laurens County. That wasn't enough for this ambitious young black man. He walked from his home in Dublin to Nashville, Tennessee, to attend Meharry Medical School. He graduated in 1897 with a medical degree, taking first place in anatomy.

On one of his walks back and forth between Dublin and Nashville, Benjamin Simmons met his future wife, Clementine Slater, who was living in Milledgeville. After his graduation, they were married in Flagg Chapel church. He passed the Georgia state board of examiners and set up his practice, becoming the first black medical doctor in Milledgeville in approximately 1897.

He was acknowledged by the local medical professionals as being well up on his knowledge of medicine. He confined most of his practice to the black community. However, in 1903 he was recognized by the white physicians when he was asked to sign their new fee schedule. He was well known as a fine diagnostician. In 1903, the *Atlanta Journal-Constitution* commented that he was very successful and could compete with the other doctors in Milledgeville.

In one challenging case, a young girl was clearly dying. The parents, seeking a cure, were asking all the physicians in town to examine her. Dr. Simmons made the unusual diagnosis of the girl having swallowed a poisonous insect. He treated the girl for several days and she recovered.

Dr. Simmons avoided politics. He worked at his profession and became wealthy. When he died in January of 1910, it was said that he had accumulated an estate of $20,000. Sadly, he died as a result of a freak accident from an unintentionally self-inflicted gunshot wound.

His funeral was held at Flagg Chapel church. It was widely attended by members of both races. His tombstone in Memory Hill Cemetery was erected to his memory through a subscription among his white friends. It states that, "His success in life affords a shining example for his race." The death of B.J. Simmons deprived Milledgeville of one of the most eager, determined and promising physicians in the state.

THE MURDER OF LEMUEL SMITH

L ATE ONE NIGHT IN DECEMBER 1832, young Lemuel Smith became involved in a heated argument at one of Milledgeville's houses of prostitution on Franklin Street. Earlier, Smith had been warned that another young man, William Flournoy of Eatonton, might pick a fight with him. In a show of bravado, Smith had displayed a pistol saying that he was "ready for him."

Flournoy stated to the patrons of the establishment that Smith was "the damned rascal who insulted me at Eatonton." Flournoy then drew his pistol while shouting, "Clear the way, gentlemen!" In the following seconds, two shots were fired. Smith's pistol discharged in his pocket as he was drawing it. Flournoy's bullet went into Lemuel Smith's chest.

Lemuel Smith was mortally wounded. The doctors who examined him said that there was nothing they could do to save him. Smith's brother, Solomon, came to the scene. Lemuel told him that he had no quarrel with William Flournoy and that their disagreement was "nonsense" and to "let it go." A few hours later he was dead. He was buried in Memory Hill Cemetery but the location of the grave has been lost.

Solomon Smith was an actor by trade. He traveled the country as the leader of a small troupe playing for a few days or weeks before moving on to another town. He was determined to see that justice was brought to the man who had killed Lemuel.

William Flournoy was a wealthy young man from a prominent family in Putnam County. He retained Augustus Holmes Kenan as his lead defense attorney. It was said that Kenan charged Flournoy $1,000 in gold for his services. The first thing that Kenan did was to hire all the attorneys in Milledgeville as part of the defense team. This meant that the prosecution had to go to Macon to find an attorney to prosecute the case.

Solomon Smith quickly studied law, and was admitted to the bar, so he could assist in the prosecution of William Flournoy. During the trial, it was brought out that Lemuel Smith had been warned against Flournoy and had shown a pistol as an indication that he was prepared to fight. Solomon Smith knew then that the case was lost.

Solomon Smith called upon his acting ability and made a dramatic closing argument.

He stood in front of the defense table and, looking right at Flournoy, said,

Whatever may be the verdict of this jury, you William Flournoy, are convicted of murder by your own conscience. You know that my brother intended you no harm—that it was not in self-defense you discharged your pistol at his heart. Before God and man, I charge you with basely murdering my young brother. You tremble now and turn pale at the charge. Your peace of mind is gone, never, never to be recovered. The sleep of the innocent will never more be yours. You are a murderer; and I tell you here in this crowded court-room, at this hour of midnight, that, whether convicted or acquitted here, you will ever more carry the mark of a homicide upon your brow; and from this time forth, in this world, you will never sleep again.

The following day, after deliberating for fifteen minutes, William Flournoy was acquitted. Solomon Smith left Milledgeville.

But the story does not end here. Three years later, in Columbus, Georgia, Solomon Smith was approached by "a stooping, miserable-looking individual." It was William Flournoy. "I heard you were here," Flournoy said, "and I have been long seeking you. Do not refuse what I have to ask." Smith said he wanted nothing to do with him and tried to walk away. Flournoy followed saying, "I want you, the brother of the man I slew, to shoot me—here—right here!" Shocked, Smith refused, saying it was not his right to punish him. Flournoy replied,

It is not punishment I ask you to inflict; that I have received already, in full measure; but it is vengeance I wish you to take—vengeance for your brother's murder, and upon his murderer. I am a murderer! I know it now! Then, I endeavored to persuade myself that I committed the deed in self-defense; but I soon found out it was not so. You said, at the trial, I would never sleep more, and I never have! Not once have I slept since that terrible night when you spoke to me in the court-room. I have closed my eyes at night, as usual; I have steeped my senses in brandy until unconsciousness took the place of sleep, but that blessed sleep you drove away that night has never returned to me for one moment. My life is a burden to me. I pray you, in God's name and in your murdered brother's, to take it—take it!

Solomon walked away leaving Flournoy standing in the middle of the street shouting at him, "I will die tonight!" The next day William Flournoy's body was found. He had been shot and scalped, one of the first victims of the Creek War.

THE MURDER
OF LEWIS H. KENAN

In 1871, EVERYONE IN MILLEDGEVILLE KNEW that Lewis H. Kenan and John R. Strother were no longer friends. On a May afternoon, John Strother and Judge Peter Fair pulled up to the curb on Wayne Street in front of Moore & Company's store. Out of the store came Lewis Kenan with a double-barreled shotgun in his hands. As he fired, the barrel of the shotgun was pushed upward by a bystander. A miss. Kenan fired the second barrel but by this time the horse reared up, throwing Strother and Fair to the ground. Before he had time to reload, Kenan was restrained by concerned citizens.

Both men were prominent in Milledgeville. Kenan was the thirty-eight-year-old son of one of Georgia's most respected attorneys, Augustus Holmes Kenan. He had been elected captain of Company I, First Georgia Regulars, and had been wounded. He was a lawyer, past mayor of Milledgeville, state senator and secretary of the Georgia Senate.

John Strother was thirty-seven years old and had also served in the Confederate army. He had also been Milledgeville's sheriff, tax collector for Baldwin County and city alderman. Strother was not currently sheriff, as he had been forced to resign his position after he had shot and killed a man "as a result of some private misunderstanding" a few years before. Strother's brother- in-law, Obadiah Arnold, was elected sheriff.

This shooting incident on Wayne Street was handled by Judge Iverson L. Harris. He had both men sign an agreement stating that neither would do anything to revive the hostility between them. Kenan said that he would no longer even carry a knife for fear that doing so would violate his honor. No motive could be obtained from either man for their conflict.

This truce lasted less than two months. John Strother broke the agreement. Kenan had been on the southwest corner of Wayne and Hancock Streets talking with some friends on the afternoon of July 3, 1871. He started to walk home with an armload of packages. He traveled westbound on the south side of Hancock Street, unaware that shadowing him on the north side of the street was John Strother, who had a rifle in his hands.

As he approached the intersection with Clarke Street, Kenan angled northward across the street, still unaware that Strother was on the opposite sidewalk. When Kenan reached the middle of the street, Strother shot him in the back from a distance of about fifteen feet. The bullet pierced both lungs, his heart and exited under the left armpit, finally coming to a stop in the wood fence that used to surround the governor's mansion property.

Kenan, lying in the street, was heard to utter his last words: "John, I did not think you would treat me so." John Strother disappeared into the evening shadows. Despite a reward offered by the governor for his capture, Strother was never seen in Milledgeville again.

The motivation for the animosity between Strother and Kenan is unknown. They do have a very unusual connection, however. Lewis Kenan's parents divorced many years earlier. In 1864, at the age of fifty-nine, Augustus H. Kenan, Lewis's father, married nineteen-year-old Sarah Barnes. They remained married until Augustus's death June 2, 1870. Less than six weeks before the murder of Lewis Kenan, Sarah Barnes Kenan married John Strother in a quiet ceremony held in her house on Liberty Street. Lewis Kenan was not listed as attending the marriage of his former step-mother, and the marriage was not covered in the newspapers.

John Strother knew he would be convicted and hang for murder; several witnesses had seen him shoot Kenan. However, despite a manhunt, he was able to slip out of town. He had his friends ship him out of town in a crate. He went by rail from the old Central of Georgia Depot on West Greene Street. His destination was Louisiana.

Strother met a violent death. In November 1888, in Louisiana, he was ambushed and shot to death on the road. The story in his family is that he had taunted a man that the baby the man's wife was carrying was actually Strother's and not the husband's. A few days later this outraged husband, and several other men, including relatives of Strother's, ambushed Strother and shot him down.

Sarah Kenan, the young widow of Augustus H. Kenan, and for a short while the wife of John Strother, died in 1874 at the age of thirty. The newspapers did not carry the report of her death. The sexton of the city cemetery lists her as "Mrs. Sarah Kenan." The cause of death portion of the report is blank. Her grave is unmarked.

General Anthony Wayne
Reminds Us That History
Is Not Boring

IT IRKS ME WHEN I hear people say that history is boring—that history is just a jumble of names, dates and events that need only be memorized for a test in school and then promptly forgotten. True, there are lots of names and dates and the events may be dimmed by the mists of time. But there's the rub. Get through, or be absorbed into, those obscuring mists, and history is alive with real people, living real lives while participating in fascinating events.

Let's take a look at General Anthony Wayne, for example. Most know that Wayne Street in Milledgeville was named for him. He had something to do with the Revolutionary War, and had the nickname "Mad Anthony." If we were going to cram for that dreaded history test, we'd throw in the names of some engagements he was involved in: Brandywine, Germantown, Paoli, Stony Point and Fallen Timbers. All pretty boring, some would say. Let us take a look at his death and what came afterward. Afterward? Does this still sound boring?

General Wayne died at the military post in Erie, Pennsylvania, in December of 1796. He had been suffering from gout and died in agony at the age of fifty-one. He was buried with full military honors, wearing his uniform, in a plain wooden coffin at the foot of the flagstaff at the post's blockhouse. The top of the coffin was marked with his initials, his age and the year of his death, all in brass tacks.

Thus it remained for twelve years. In the fall of 1808, however, General Wayne's daughter Margarita was seriously ill and contemplating her own death. She suggested that her brother, thirty-seven-year-old Colonel Isaac Wayne, bring their father's bones back to the family burial plot in Radnor, Pennsylvania, which is just outside Philadelphia.

The following spring, Colonel Wayne went in a light two-wheeled cart to Erie, which is in the extreme northwest portion of the state. He arranged to have Anthony Wayne's coffin exhumed. He did not feel comfortable watching the proceedings so he left town for the day. He left in charge the same doctor who had treated Anthony Wayne in his final illness.

To the utter astonishment of the doctor, his wife and the men who were employed to dig up the coffin, the body of Anthony Wayne had not decomposed. It was in an excellent state of preservation with the exception of one leg and foot that were partially gone.

Clearly, the body could not be removed to Radnor, Pennsylvania. The doctor's solution to the problem was to boil the body in water thus enabling him to separate the flesh from the bones, then the bones could be packed in a trunk for their journey to the new burial location in Radnor.

There were at least four assistants as well as spectators who watched the proceedings. The wife of the commandant of the post said later that the body had the appearance of plaster of Paris and was not hard but rather more the consistency of soft chalk.

One enterprising man noticed that the remaining boot, the other having disintegrated along with the foot, appeared to be the same size as his own. He took possession of the boot and had a boot maker create a match for it. He wore his "new" boots until they wore out.

A large kettle was obtained in which to boil the body. The kettle was not large enough so the body was cut into pieces of convenient sizes and then dropped into the boiling water. As the flesh separated from the bones it was carved away by the doctor and his assistants who scraped the bones clean. The bones were then packed in a trunk. The water in the kettle, along with the flesh, knives and instruments used in the operation, were put back into the coffin in the original grave.

Isaac Wayne regretted the decision to handle his father's body in such a manner. Had he known of the state of preservation he would have preferred to have left the body in Erie and erect a monument there to his father's memory. But now he had no choice but to take the bones back to Radnor for reburial.

On June 5, 1811, the Pennsylvania State Society of the Cincinnati put a monument over the grave that still stands, though it is badly weathered. The ceremony was very elaborate. The procession to the cemetery at St. David's Episcopal Church was a mile long. Old soldiers and dignitaries attended in huge numbers.

In Erie, Pennsylvania, the historical society exhibits a kettle they claim was the kettle used to process the body. It has been a major attraction for almost a hundred years. The original grave is marked with a tombstone.

Opinions about this look at Anthony Wayne will certainly vary. However, I suspect few would describe it as boring. That's the real point—history isn't boring.

General Nathanael
Greene's Hat

MY DOCTOR ONCE TALKED TO me about the sun, skin cancer and sunstroke. He asked if I wore a hat. I replied that I often wore a baseball cap. He said, "That's not a hat." I immediately thought of General Nathanael Greene's hat.

Despite being a household name in the American Revolution, Nathanael Greene today is not well remembered. In Milledgeville, we have Greene Street and to the north is Greene County. However, the man himself is pretty obscure to most of us.

Like most of the Patriot commanders, Greene had no formal military training. Before the war, he ran his father's iron foundry in Rhode Island. A Quaker, he was reprimanded in 1773 when he attended a military parade. He learned his military skills before the war from books. Later, he learned on the job by making mistakes and learning from them. In 1774, he helped raise a militia company called the Kentish Guards, which he joined as a private.

In 1775, the state of Rhode Island raised three regiments and promoted him from private to brigadier general to command them. A few months later, at the siege of Boston, he was made a brigadier general in the Continental army. He was then thirty-four years old.

The major tactical disaster of his career was his decision to try to hold Fort Washington on Manhattan Island in 1776. After a short battle, the fort was forced to surrender its garrison of three thousand men and huge quantities of supplies. In the following months, he did well during the retreat of Washington's army across New Jersey and the Delaware River. He commanded one of the wings of George Washington's army during the spectacularly successful attack on Trenton and a week later during the battle of Princeton. In both battles, Greene was conspicuous by his exposure to enemy fire as he led his men from the front. In September and October, Greene again competently led his men in the battles of Brandywine and Germantown.

In 1780, Patriot General Horatio Gates was overwhelmed at the battle of Camden by Lord Cornwallis. Not only was his army routed, but Gates fled the field. In fact, he covered 180 miles in three days, leaving his infantry to fend for themselves. As Alexander Hamilton wryly commented about Gates's precipitous flight, "It does admirable credit to the activity of a man at his time of life." After the disaster at Camden, the war in the South looked lost.

Washington, however, wasn't going to concede the South to the British. He dispatched General Greene with the urgent assignment of restoring an army in the South and giving battle to Cornwallis. General Greene, now with an independent command, rushed to North Carolina. He not only rallied the beaten and leaderless remnants of Gates's army but also recruited new men. He established a supply system. Most importantly, he conceived a strategy that would in the end defeat Lord Cornwallis.

The plan was risky. Greene split his forces into widely separated groups. Greene also would retreat when faced with superior forces. This would compel Cornwallis to divide up his larger army to protect a vast area of South Carolina and North Carolina. Greene's forces would then engage in small battles and through attrition wear Cornwallis down. This also had the advantage of not risking everything in large battles where he might lose his entire army.

While Greene never won a major battle, he did not lose the campaign. Eventually, Cornwallis was drawn into Virginia where he finally was cornered at Yorktown. Greene said, "there are few generals that have run oftener, or more lustily than I have done. But I have taken care not to run too far, and commonly have run as fast forward as backward, to convince the Enemy that we were like a Crab, that could run either way." He summed up his strategy and the spirit of his men saying, "we fight, get beat, rise, and fight again."

After the war, the grateful state of Georgia gave a plantation near Savannah, which had belonged to the Loyalist lieutenant governor of Georgia, to Greene in recognition of his services. He lived there for only a year. In June of 1786, he was visiting a neighboring plantation and spent the day walking around under the hot sun. Finally, we come to the matter of General Greene's hat. He wasn't wearing a hat that day. He became ill on the way home and died the following day of sunstroke. He was forty-four years old.

FLYING OVER MILLEDGEVILLE, 1877 STYLE

PEOPLE FLY OVER MILLEDGEVILLE EVERY day. It's no big deal. People have been doing it for decades. In the last sixty years, airplanes in the sky have become common. Even seventy-five years ago, airplanes, while still causing people to stop and look skyward, were not something really extraordinary. However, any airplane that appeared in the sky over central Georgia before 1925 was a rarity and cause for comment. The first airplane to appear over Milledgeville probably did so around 1915.

To Hiram Plattney goes the honor of being the first man to fly over Milledgeville. But, he didn't do it in 1915. In fact, his flight was twenty-six years before the Wright Brothers flew the first airplane at Kitty Hawk, North Carolina, in 1903. Hiram Plattney didn't use an airplane. He flew a balloon. It was a cold, wet and slushy January day in 1877 when Hiram Plattney's balloon ascended from Milledgeville. It would be standard to say that Plattney was at the controls of the craft. But he wasn't. In fact, he wasn't actually in the basket hanging under the balloon, either. Plattney was more of a showman than that.

Hiram Plattney went aloft hanging by one hand to a trapeze bar dangling from beneath the basket. Not content with that he also hung from this bar by his feet "after reaching a frightful height." He passed over the State House (Old Capital Building) and then crossed over the Oconee River. He landed safely on the plantation of a Captain Jones.

A large crowd had stood, impatiently, in the cold for several hours waiting to witness this spectacle. The local newspaper took a dim view of the proceedings, suggesting that a few dollars and a minute's applause was a poor reward for Plattney to have risked his life.

Although the name of Hiram Plattney is not immortalized on an historic marker on State House square, he does have a legitimate right to a certain amount of fame. He is the first man to view Milledgeville from the air and the first to fly over the State House. He also is likely the only person who has ever flown over Milledgeville while hanging by his feet. That is a record that probably will never be equaled.

THE GWINNETT-
MCINTOSH DUEL

YOU ARE A SCOUNDREL AND a lying rascal," announced General Lachlan McIntosh in front of the Georgia State Assembly on May 15, 1777. He was speaking to his longtime rival Button Gwinnett. Gwinnett discussed the ramifications of the statement with his close colleagues and concluded that his honor could only be restored by challenging McIntosh to a duel. The invitation was made and accepted. The contest was to be the following morning at dawn.

The friction between Gwinnett and McIntosh was one of long standing and concerned their respective roles in the Georgia military during the Revolutionary War. Gwinnett was elected commander of Georgia's Continental battalion in 1776. His election was controversial, so he resigned and was appointed one of Georgia's representatives to the Continental Congress, which was meeting in Philadelphia. Lachlan McIntosh was placed in command of the Georgia Continental troops as brigadier general, replacing Gwinnett.

Gwinnett signed the Declaration of Independence in August of 1776 and soon after returned to Georgia. He was elected speaker of Georgia's Provincial Congress and later president and commander in chief of Georgia's forces. He tried to rid the military of those he thought were unfit to hold high rank. One of these was Lachlan McIntosh's brother George, whom Gwinnett had arrested for treason and thrown into jail. George McIntosh was later exonerated, but there were considerable hard feelings over the arrest on the part of Lachlan McIntosh.

Gwinnett had a desire to prove that he had military abilities. He organized an expedition against St. Augustine. McIntosh wouldn't cooperate with him and the expedition bogged down as they squabbled. The Georgia Council of Safety ordered both men to return to Savannah and allowed Colonel Samuel Elbert to take command in the field. The expedition failed.

The Georgia Assembly investigated the activities of Gwinnett on the expedition and approved his conduct. It was then that General McIntosh spoke his "fightin'" words that brought on the duel.

At dawn, on May 16, 1777, forty-two-year-old Button Gwinnett and his second walked onto the meadow near Savannah where the duel was to take place. Lachlan McIntosh, wearing his dress uniform, was already there, accompanied by his second. As had been arranged by the seconds, McIntosh furnished the pistols. They were a finely designed identical pair of dueling pistols. If I were Button Gwinnett, I would have had second thoughts at about this time. A man who possesses dueling pistols, like the man with a custom pool cue, is likely to know how to use them.

The four men made polite greetings to one another but did not discuss the cause of their meeting. The dueling pistols were given to Gwinnett and his second to inspect. The pistols were then loaded in full view so nothing underhanded could take place. A short discussion followed as to the distance the men would stand from each other. Gwinnett said that he'd be happy with "whatever distance the General pleases." General McIntosh suggested eight or ten feet. The seconds agreed to four paces, which would be about eleven or twelve feet. The seconds suggested that the men face away from each other and when given the command would turn and fire. McIntosh objected, saying, "by no means, let us see what we are about."

So, it came down to the rivals standing four paces apart, facing each other, with their arms hanging at their sides, pistols pointed at the ground. In an attempt to redeem his honor, Gwinnett found himself facing an armed foe at a distance where he could see not only the whites of McIntosh's eyes, but also his eyelashes. His opponent, the fifty-year-old general, stared into Gwinnett's brown eyes and for a brief instant wondered if he was a fool to have insulted the man in public. A second shouted, "fire!" Both men raised their arms and fired simultaneously. Gwinnett fell to the ground, grasping his leg saying, "my thigh is broken." McIntosh was also wounded in the leg but remained on his feet.

McIntosh called out to Gwinnett inquiring if he'd care to reload and continue the contest. Gwinnett replied that he'd be glad to continue if someone would help him stand up. At that time the seconds got between the men and refused to allow a second shot. The seconds agreed that honor was satisfied.

Lachlan McIntosh recovered slowly. Button Gwinnett's wound became infected and then gangrenous. He died within three days.

McIntosh was tried for murder and acquitted. However, he was so unpopular among the supporters of Gwinnett that he was transferred to George Washington's army in Pennsylvania. He was later transferred to command of the Western Department where he was successful in leading an expedition against the Indians who were allied with the British in the Ohio Valley. He returned to Savannah after the war. He was a delegate to the Continental Congress from Georgia in 1784. He died in 1806 at the age of seventy-nine.

In Milledgeville, we remember General Lachlan McIntosh with a street named in his honor. There is also a McIntosh County named for him.

Button Gwinnett should be remembered by all of us on the chance that we may come upon his autograph. It is sought by collectors, as he was a signer of the Declaration of Independence. However, as he died less than a year after signing the Declaration, his autograph is one of the rarest of the rare and worth well over $100,000. Button Gwinnett is also remembered with a county in Georgia and a street in Milledgeville. That street has now changed its name to honor Martin Luther King.

THE VOODOO MURDERS

In the spring of 1887, Milledgeville was shocked to learn that an entire family, eleven in all, were dead or at the point of death. What captivated the local population, and newspapers across the country, was the suggestion that the cause of the illness was voodoo.

John Harris lived with his wife and nine children at Brown's Crossing. They ate a meal together and all became sick. They were sick to the point of becoming unconscious. The first death was a child. Dr. John Hardeman was called and he suspected poison. He removed the child's stomach and turned it over to Dr. I.L. Harris for examination. Dr. Harris was assisted by druggist George D. Case and Professor D.H. Hill Jr. of the college. They could find no trace of poison.

The story gets even more interesting as it was said that John Harris had a dispute with his brother-in-law, Jim Bonner. Jim Bonner was said to be a practitioner of voodoo, and the dispute was whether or not Bonner had unexplained powers. Bonner was reported to have said that because John Harris did not believe in the power of voodoo, his entire family would die within a month.

Three of John Harris's children died the same night and the fourth died the next day. Just after their funeral, their mother died. John Harris became a raving maniac, suffering from frightful visions. He was placed in the State Lunatic Asylum. The other children were not expected to recover.

C.W. Ennis, the Milledgeville police chief, immediately arrested Jim Bonner on suspicion of murder. Bonner had married a sister of Mrs. Harris. He had a reputation of being a voodoo doctor and was held in awe by many. It was said that he used roots and medicinal plants that he gathered in the woods and swamps to make potions. Harris had openly ridiculed Bonner when he claimed that he would take frogs out of the legs of poisoned people. Bonner became furious. He was kept a short time in jail, but as there was no real evidence against him he was released. He and his wife went to Putnam County but did not attempt to flee the area.

The stomach from the mother was removed and sent to Athens by Judge D.B. Sanford to the Georgia State chemist Professor H.C. White for examination.

After only a day or two at the Asylum, Harris died in convulsions. Rumors were sweeping the county that Bonner had once been consulted by a woman looking for a love powder to give her husband who had left her. The powder was later found to be a poison. Another story had Bonner treating a sick woman who died. A physician who saw her before she died said he believed she died of poison, although the body was never tested for poison.

The results of the examination of the stomach came back from Professor White. It did nothing to clear up the mystery. No evidence of poison was found in the contents of the stomach. Professor White did state, however, that death may result from the "eating of decayed meat, toad stools, milk or cheese rendered poisoned by fermentation etc., no evidence of which may be discovered in the body after death by chemical analysis."

This response from Professor White was unsatisfactory. His analysis only eliminated the possibility of poison. He suggested the possibility of spoiled food but supplied no evidence of its existence in this case. With no evidence to support the hypothesis that the six members of the Harris family had died of poison or that they had ingested spoiled food, many believed that the real murder weapon was voodoo.

With nothing other than rumors of ill will and wild talk of voodoo, a criminal case could not be brought against Jim Bonner. He was never brought to trial. The six deaths remain an unsolved mystery. Bonner may have been entirely innocent or perhaps he had committed the perfect crime through the use of voodoo. Who can say for sure?

GET YOUR HEAD EXAMINED

PHRENOLOGY, THE STUDY OF THE physical external structure of the human skull to determine a person's character and mental capability, was all the rage in the mid 1800s. The word itself comes from the Greek roots *phren*, meaning "mind," and *logos*, meaning "study."

The basic idea behind phrenology was the belief that the surface of the brain was composed of as many as thirty-five "organs." These organs controlled such things as emotions, intellectual aptitude, propensities for good and evil, theft or murder, self-esteem and benevolence. The organs that were used got bigger and those that were not used tended to shrink. The skull would reflect these differences by slight bumps or depressions. Charts were devised that would be used like a map to indicate the areas of the skull over the various brain organs.

Phrenology became popular in England in the early 1800s and spread to the United States. Phrenology societies sprang up, lecturers spoke to huge audiences as people began to feel they had found an explanation for many of the unknowable facets of life. Scientists and well-educated people seriously studied the surfaces of their own skulls, their friends' and the public's, as well as the skulls of criminals and the insane. The phrenologist would run his finger tips, or sometimes the flat of the hand, across the skull, carefully noting any irregularities. Sometimes calipers and measuring tapes were used to create a detailed chart of the skull of the client. It is hard to understand the initial popularity of phrenology among scientists as there is virtually no empirical evidence for a relationship between bumps or depressions on the skull and character or personality traits.

It wasn't long before charlatans and con men entered the field. The scientists eventually drifted away and phrenology became the domain of the fast talking, slick entrepreneur who would "read a head" for a fee.

Such a man visited Milledgeville in the fall of 1845. "J. Anton, Practical Phrenologist" took a room at the McComb Hotel, which was located on the southwest corner of Greene and Wayne Streets. He advertised that he "respectfully informs the citizens of Milledgeville, members of the Legislature, and all visitors" that he was "prepared to measure and make examinations of heads, and give correct Phrenological Charts of the character and talents of those who may honor him with their patronage."

This service came at a price. Two dollars would get the client an examination of the skull and a chart of the owner's character and talents. However, discounts would be offered if an entire family requested examination. There was also a deduction "when a club of gentlemen have their heads examined at one time." Two dollars then is equal to about forty dollars in today's money; so it wasn't an insignificant sum.

There is no way to know how many people took advantage of Mr. Anton's offer. He was in Milledgeville for at least two months and maybe many more. It would be fascinating to see the list of his clients who had endured having their skulls measured, charted and thoroughly fingered by Mr. Anton. It would also be interesting to know what the local physicians and educated people thought of his talents.

While phrenology went out of favor in the latter part of the nineteenth century, it did not, and has not, gone away entirely. The British Phrenological Society did not disband until 1967. Even today there are active Phrenological societies and people seriously promoting the practice. I don't believe, however, there is a "practical phrenologist" in Milledgeville eager to examine our heads at the present time.

OLD MILLEDGEVILLE LAMAR MYTH
REPLACED WITH FACT

H ISTORY IS FULL OF MYTHS and legends. Some, like George Washington and the cherry tree, are entirely false. Others, such as George Washington's wooden dentures, are partly true—George Washington had dentures, but never wooden ones.

Milledgeville has such myths and legends, too. There is the one about the tunnel between the governor's mansion and the State House, for example. There is also the myth about Judge L.Q.C. Lamar's death.

The basic myth story is that in July 1834, Lucius Quintus Cincinnatus Lamar, judge of the Ocmulgee Circuit, committed suicide in a fit of melancholy. His melancholy was brought about because of a murder trial in which a man, who was a Methodist minister, was accused of having killed his wife's young sister. The wife was the principle witness against the accused man. The evidence was circumstantial but the man was convicted. Judge Lamar sentenced him to death and the guilty man was hanged. Later, a condemned man on the gallows in another state admitted to the murder. Judge Lamar believed he had executed an innocent man and, in his despair, Lamar committed suicide.

This myth has been circulating for well over a century. It has been repeated so often that long ago it took on the mantle of truth. The myth can by found in reputable Georgia history books and books about the famous Lamar family. Respected historians repeat it as gospel. The trouble is, it's not true.

When I initiated my research, I was not looking at Judge Lamar at all, as I assumed the story to be true. I wanted to find information on the murder and subsequent trial. Information was extremely limited. The name of the alleged murderer was not even known, nor that of his victim. Even the year of the murder was unknown. Primary sources were very skimpy. Secondary sources, history books and articles all basically repeated the same old story with very few details and never cited primary sources.

Incredibly, a transcript of the murder trial was located. Now, with further research, the real story could be told for the first time in 170 years.

On November 13, 1832, twelve-year-old Elenor Bustin was strangled to death with a cotton cord. Her older sister, Nancy, was the wife of John Johnson, a part-time minister. Elenor was found in a hackberry bush in the woods with the cord around her neck. Evidence from those who discovered the body revealed that she had not hanged herself in an apparent suicide, as her feet were touching the ground. Rather, she was choked to death by an unknown third party. Evidence, all of it circumstantial, began to accumulate around the minister. He could not account for his whereabouts at the time of the murder, and he had been known to berate and even to beat the young girl. But there was no real motive and no evidence to put him at the scene of the crime.

Johnson was arrested. He was indicted by the grand jury. The jurors were Samuel Boykin, David B. Hill, Edmond Horton, Bartley McCrary, William D. Jarratt, Levin J. Smith, Robert McCombs, Richard M. Orme, Baradel P. Stubbs, Shadrack Bivins, George A. Brown, Richard Pickett, John B. Dyer, John M. Carter, Isham Reddy, Thomas H. Hall, Henry Duncan, Levi Speights, Jacob Fogle, Isaac T. Cushing and Pryor Wright.

Johnson plead innocent at his trial. Some believed that he acted in a suspicious manner, however. At his trial, his wife did not testify against him. She did not testify at all. His neighbors testified against him but without providing solid evidence. The jury convicted him of murder. The jurors at his trial were William D. Ray, David Collins, Mark Brown, James Young, Matthew Brewer, Francis Pemberton, Solomon Robinson, Charles Atcheson, Joseph West, John Prosser, John Kirkpatrick and Jacob P. Turner.

The law allowed Judge Lamar only one sentence he could impose: hanging. Many thought that as the case was based entirely upon circumstantial evidence, Johnson should be given life in prison. However, the law did not allow such a sentence. The hanging was postponed for a week or two while the state legislature debated the issue of circumstantial evidence and whether or not Johnson should be pardoned. In the end, the legislature failed to act. A few days later on November 27, 1833, Johnson was hanged, still proclaiming his innocence from the gallows.

The newspapers of the time indicate that Judge Lamar suffered from what would be called today extreme depression. On July 4, 1834, he took his own life, but at the time there was no mention of this murder case having anything to do with the depression or the suicide. In fact, no mention was made of any case troubling him.

The first suggestion that the wrong man may have been hanged surfaced ten years later in 1843. An anonymous letter, signed by "Justice," appeared in newspapers stating that "an act of injustice" had been done to the family of "the unfortunate Mr. Johnston [sic]," who had been hanged for the murder of his sister-in-law. The letter asked that the legislature "make some donation for the support of the family of this unfortunate man."

The anonymous letter went on to say that an unnamed "gentleman traveling from Alabama, put up at the Union Hall in Forsyth, and in a conversation he had with the proprietor of the house, stated that a Negro fellow had been taken up for having committed violence upon the body of a white female." In the course of his interrogation, this unnamed black man additionally confessed to killing the girl for whose murder Johnson was hanged in Milledgeville.

Clearly, Judge Lamar had no way of knowing that the man he had sentenced to death might have been innocent, as ten years had passed before there was any indication that another person may have been connected with the crime. Also, one wonders how much weight he would have put on an anonymous letter from a party that does not give any identification as to who the confessed murderer was, other than he was an unnamed man somewhere in Alabama.

For over one hundred years, whenever capital punishment or circumstantial evidence was discussed in the press, this Baldwin County murder was brought up with the added feature that the famed Judge L.Q.C. Lamar had committed suicide after learning that the "real" murderer had confessed. The story has become ingrained into the history of Milledgeville and Georgia.

We will never know what demons tormented Judge Lamar to the point that he took his own life. We can say, for sure, that it was not the knowledge that he had hanged an innocent man. The old myth will no doubt live on in Milledgeville and in Georgia history. It would take a pen mightier than mine to lay it to rest. However, now when we run into the myth, we will know the facts it obscures.

A Cure for the Common Scold

IN THE 1600s AND 1700s, courts in England and the American colonies legally punished women for the crime of being a "common scold."

It was, and is, somewhat vague as to just what one needed to do to become a common scold. A legal definition advises us that the term applies to "a woman, who, in consequence of her boisterous, disorderly and quarrelsome tongue, is a public nuisance to the neighborhood. Such a woman may be indicted, and on conviction, punished. At common law, the punishment was by being placed in a certain engine of correction called the trebucket or ducking stool."

The "engine of correction" used to punish these women with quarrelsome tongues could be of various designs but the general idea is that of a "see-saw." It would be constructed along a convenient river bank, pond or lake. At one end of the see-saw would be a chair and the other end a long handle. The convicted woman would be tied to the chair and ducked into the water several times, as ordered by the court, "to cool her immoderate heat."

Milledgeville has never been on the cutting edge of ducking stool technology. In fact, we have never had a ducking stool of any kind. That doesn't mean, however, that we did not indulge in the great spectator sport of ducking boisterous and disorderly women.

About 195 years ago, an old woman by the name of Miss Palmer lived in Milledgeville. She apparently was such an annoyance to her neighbors, with her "glib tongue," that charges were brought against her. She was indicted, tried and convicted of being a common scold by the superior court of Baldwin County. Judge Peter Early sentenced her to be ducked three times in the Oconee River.

Instead of having the taxpayers of Baldwin County build a ducking chair for the occasion, a suitable, and free, alternative was arranged. Miss Palmer was tied to the back of a cart by Major Phil Cook, the sheriff. Accompanied by a hooting mob, she was taken to the river, where the cart was run down into the water. After holding her under water for some seconds the cart was pulled out. As the unruly Miss Palmer regained the atmosphere, she exclaimed with great gravity, "Glory to God!" She was ducked a second and a third time as ordered by the judge. Each time as she came to the surface she would shout "Glory to God!"

Apparently, Miss Palmer's "immoderate heat" was not cooled by the waters of the Oconee River. Perhaps, despite Milledgeville's citizens' obvious enjoyment of the spectacle, the failure to rectify Miss Palmer's behavior is why we no longer engage in ducking boisterous and disorderly women with quarrelsome tongues.

MILLEDGEVILLE READING ROOM

TODAY WE TAKE HAVING A library for granted. It was not always so. In 1820, the "Milledgeville Reading Room" opened. Unlike the public libraries of today, the Milledgeville Reading Room was available only by subscription. The cost was six dollars per year, roughly equivalent to sixty-nine dollars in today's money. Non-permanent residents, such as legislators, could pay by the month.

The unknown proprietor made available books, as well as forty to fifty titles of magazines and newspapers, providing "a view of almost every thing worth notice passing in the world; its literature, religion, arts, policy, agriculture, commerce, news, anecdote, etc. and the discussion of those topics that interest or agitate the human family, delineated by the hands of masters." Magazines included *Ackerman's Elegant Repository of the Arts*, *North American Review*, *American Farmer*, *Portfolio*, *Christian Observer* and *Medical Recorder*. Newspapers included *Richmond Enquirer*, *National Intelligencer*, *National Advocate*, *National Gazette*, *Darien Gazette* and *Savannah Republican*. None of the materials in the Reading Room would be lent to the subscribers, but had to be enjoyed on the premises.

The need for such an establishment was thought to be required by "the ingenious mechanic, the intelligent farmer, the professional man, and the man of business." These men were invited to "enjoy the desultory half hour of needful relaxation, to increase his stores of valuable information, his acquaintance with books, authors, wit, poetry, etc. and his taste, excitement and materials for interesting reflection and enlightened conversation."

Nowhere are women mentioned in connection with the Reading Room. Perhaps it would be unseemly for a woman to want to read these publications. Or, maybe a woman of refinement would not want to visit an establishment frequented by the men of Milledgeville. This may be especially true as the Milledgeville Reading Room advertised that "refreshments of the best description, will be kept in readiness." Just what these refreshments were has been lost to history.

It is interesting that after 184 years, Georgia College & State University Library has followed the lead of the Milledgeville Reading Room in making refreshments available for its patrons. However, I'm sure the 1820s patrons would be stunned at the two-dollar cup of Starbucks coffee now offered at GCSU's library. Mary Vinson Memorial Library, perhaps to its credit, has not yet gotten on the 1820s refreshment bandwagon.

Neither of our major libraries can compete with the Milledgeville Reading Room when it comes to hours of operation. Mary Vinson Library is open during the week a total of fifty-one hours. GCSU's library does only slightly better at fifty-two hours. The Milledgeville Reading Room was open 7:00 a.m. until 9:00 p.m., for a total of seventy hours in a five-day week. It is unknown what hours, if any, the Milledgeville Reading Room was open on Saturday and Sunday.

Milledgeville's first library is, of course, no longer in existence. Its physical location and date when it closed its doors for the last time has been lost. The Reading Room lives on in spirit, however, in our current libraries. Perhaps, on some dark and moonless night, a wandering lost soul will appear in the doorway of one of our libraries and ask for the latest copy of *Ackerman's Elegant Repository of the Arts*.

SALUBRIOUS MILLEDGEVILLE...
OR IS IT?

IN THE VERY EARLY DAYS, Milledgeville was thought by many to be an unhealthy place. Because Milledgeville was the new state capital, it was welcome news in 1817 when it was announced that the mortality rate was actually quite low. At that time, the population of Milledgeville was 1,700, having increased by about 550 persons since 1810. In 1816, 24 people died in Milledgeville, which works out to be about 1 in 70, or, as modern mortality tables would state it, a rate of 1,428 deaths per 100,000 people.

This rate compared favorably with that of New York City, which at the time had a mortality rate of 2,500 deaths per 100,000. The rates of death in European cities were all significantly higher than Milledgeville. It was also stated, but no figures given, that Milledgeville's mortality rate had been stable for the past three years. It was also proudly pointed out that not one adult death was a result of "Bilious Fever." Bilious Fever was the name given to malarial fevers and typhoid. Clearly, Milledgeville was a healthy place to live—far better than most at the time. In fact, it was stated that "few places, in the same latitude, are more salubrious than Milledgeville."

Before we get carried away, however, we should take a look at the mortality rates in modern times. We find that Baldwin County in 2003 had a mortality rate of 914 deaths per 100,000. That's considerably better than 1,428 deaths per 100,000 in 1816. But, after almost two hundred years of improved medical care and sanitation we ought to expect significant improvement.

Baldwin County's 914 deaths per 100,000 doesn't look quite so rosy when compared to the state of Georgia as a whole, which in 2003 had a death rate of 763 per 100,000. It looks even less attractive when compared to New York City, which in 2003 had a rate of 750 deaths per 100,000 population.

I am not suggesting that there is anything amiss with the medical treatment or sanitation of Milledgeville. It would take one far more knowledgeable than I to explain these figures. I can say, however, with some certainty, that last year Milledgeville did not have any deaths due to Bilious Fever.

THE KILLING OF DEPUTY MARSHAL
CHARLES HAYGOOD

THE EARLY SPRING OF 1886 was a time of turmoil in Milledgeville. Baldwin County was to vote on whether it should be dry or wet. The prohibition issue divided the town and even divided families. Strong feelings were held on both sides of the question. Passionate speeches were made on street corners to equally passionate listeners. Tension was high.

About 5:00 p.m. on Saturday, February 27, 1886, thirty-year-old Deputy Marshal Charles N. Haygood was on duty near the corner of Wayne and Hancock Streets. P.T. Ennis, known as "Doshe" to his friends, was standing on a cotton bale giving a speech favoring the anti-prohibition position. A brother of Doshe, twenty-seven-year-old Elias N. Ennis, known as "Sam," walked past Haygood just as he was speaking to another man in the crowd.

Words were exchanged between Sam Ennis and Charles Haygood. But just what was said was not heard by any of the numerous witnesses. Ennis then walked away with another man. Haygood approached Ennis and spoke to him again, and they walked together toward the sidewalk on the south side of Hancock Street, about fifty feet west of Wayne Street. Suddenly, Ennis pulled a pistol and placed it against the left side of Haygood's chest and fired. He immediately fired a second shot into Haygood's left chest. Haygood turned and ran toward the corner of Hancock and Wayne. Ennis fired a third shot at Haygood's back but missed.

Haygood turned the corner onto Wayne Street and ran about a hundred yards down the sidewalk to the drugstore of C.L. Case. This store was located in the building where Edward Jones Investments is now located, at 131 South Wayne. Clearly, Haygood was seeking medical attention. Drs. J.M. Whitaker, Powell, Callaway, Sims and Smith attempted to save him. Haygood said, "Why did he do it? I have never harmed him." In about thirty minutes he was dead. One of the bullets had gone through his heart and another went into his left lung.

Sam Ennis immediately surrendered himself to the sheriff, his brother C.W. Ennis. After taking him into custody, Sheriff Ennis distanced himself from the case and allowed his marshals to take charge of his brother.

Charles Haygood was buried in Memory Hill Cemetery the following day with a large crowd in attendance. He was a member of the Baldwin Blues, who fired a salute over his grave. He was also a member of the Royal Arcanum Lodge 375. The pallbearers—Yoel Joel, C.P. Crawford, Ed. Beub, H.W. Bass, James Supple, Carlos G. Wilson, Jacob Caraker and A.L. Ellison—were Royal Arcanum members. The Royal Arcanum was a life insurance society, which paid Haygood's widow, Dixie Haygood, $3,000.

On March 2, the city council passed an ordinance prohibiting any further street speechmaking. The coroner's jury indicted Sam Ennis for murder. At the preliminary trial during the first week of March, two witnesses were presented for the prosecution. The defense produced no witnesses but submitted a statement by Sam Ennis giving his version of the shooting. The prosecution was handled by Sam Jemison, W.A. Lofton and C.P. Crawford. Ennis was represented by Seaborn Reese, Judge D.B. Sanford and J.T. Allen. Judge Ramsey bound Ennis over to the superior court but reduced the charge from murder to manslaughter. Bail was set at $2,500. Ennis posted bail and was released.

Sam Ennis's statement, the only account of the exchange of words between himself and Haygood, makes a case for self-defense. In it, Ennis says that he overheard Haygood say that his brother, Doshe Ennis, "was a regular damned shit arse." Sam Ennis asked Haygood what he meant by that remark, and he claims that Haygood replied that Doshe "was a nice man but had no argument." Ennis says he then left Haygood and walked a short distance on Hancock Street when Haygood came up and asked to speak with him as they walked. Ennis claimed that Haygood said to him, with his right hand in his hip pocket where he kept his

DIXIE HAYGOOD AND THE MAGIC OF HER ANNIE ABBOTT ACT

revolver, "by God, if you go where I want you to go, it will be the end of you." Ennis said that he saw Haygood try to pull his revolver. Ennis then pulled out his own revolver and fired "three shots as quick as I could…As I fired the 3rd shot he seemed to be turning away."

The trial was held on August 12, 1886. It was the second murder trial in Baldwin's new courthouse. The trial lasted all day. After "a short absence" the jury brought in a verdict of "not guilty." The prosecution was represented by Solicitor General Whitfield and the defense by Seaborn Reese, D.B. Sanford and J.F. Little. The jurors were W.R. Fenn, Thomas Smith, E.H. Thomas, John Scogin, A.F. Wynne, U.M. Erwin, J.W. Goodson, W.J. Tucker, Dawson Wilkinson, Warren Edwards, C.M. Gibson and Joel Goddard.

Sam Ennis lived a long and successful life. He was in the mercantile business in Washington county. However, his wife and children lived in Milledgeville. He was a director on the board of the First National Bank and was also a vice president and later president of the bank. He had a reputation of being an honest man. He died in 1936. He is buried in Memory Hill Cemetery.

Charles Haygood was survived by his mother, a brother William and his wife Dixie Jarratt Haygood and three children. After a few years, Dixie went on the road performing a magic act under the name of Annie Abbott, the Little Georgia Magnet, until her death in 1915. She made a fortune and her fame was worldwide. She is buried in Memory Hill next to her husband.

O NE OF THE UNFOUNDED LEGENDS of Milledgeville, which will apparently continue forever, is annually revived and renewed by people who should know better. It's the legend of Dixie Haygood, the alleged witch of Milledgeville. This much-maligned woman was not a witch. She was a magician and a highly skilled and successful one, too.

Her husband, Deputy Marshal Charles N. Haygood, was shot and killed on Hancock Street in February of 1886, leaving Dixie with three children. The youngest child, Charles Jr., was only a few weeks old.

A year or two earlier, the famed Lulu Hurst, the Georgia Wonder, toured through central Georgia, stopping at Milledgeville. Undoubtedly, her act was seen by Dixie and Charles. Lulu Hurst claimed to have an unexplained power that would allow her to defy the combined strength of several men. She would conduct "tests," or tricks, where she would have men hold objects such as chairs, an umbrella or billiard cue. With a touch of her hands, the "power" would start the object moving and the man, or men, would be unable to hold the object still and would be thrown around the stage. Within weeks, Dixie was performing similar, some said better, routines at the Opera House on Hancock Street and in nearby towns. A couple of years after Charles's death, Dixie Haygood, having perfected her own tricks, went on the road doing performances in Georgia and nearby states.

Soon, Dixie Haygood started using "Annie Abbott" as her stage name. She appended "the Little Georgia Magnet" to her title, which added a flair and bit of mystery. While Lulu Hurst was a large and muscular fifteen-year-old, Dixie Haygood was a trim ninety-eight pounds. This made her apparent ability to withstand the strongest men an even better show than that of Lulu Hurst.

The trademark of the Annie Abbott act was the "lift test." Strong men would be invited from the audience and asked to attempt to lift her. When she wanted to be lifted, the men would easily lift her into the air. However, when she exerted her "power" she was unliftable. She also performed a test where she would hold a billiard cue horizontally in her open hands. Several men would be asked to push, together, against the billiard cue. Annie Abbott, standing on one foot, would resist their combined efforts. These and similar "strength" demonstrations were very dramatic and caused a great stir in the scientific community.

Dixie Haygood, or Annie Abbott as she now called herself, did not say she was a magician. She offered no explanation for the apparently mysterious "power" that enabled her to do her act. Many scientists accepted her at face value and struggled to find an explanation for her apparently inexplicable strength. She was subjected to many examinations by eminent physicians. While she would be performing, they would take her temperature, heart rate, feel her muscles and have her stand on a scale. They even examined her clothing and the floor on which she stood. Many in the scientific community were convinced that she had a power never before known to man. They wrote long studies of her in scientific journals.

Of course, there was no unknown power involved in her act. She made clever use of leverage and the center of gravity in her performances to make it appear that she had superior strength when compared to the strong men she "overpowered." Frequently, the solution to her tricks would be published by newspapers, magazines or scientific journals. But this never seemed to diminish her appeal with the public. One can only wonder at the stage presence and personal charisma of the little lady magician to carry off such elementary stunts in front of so many people for so long.

The attention shown by the doctors and scientists enhanced her career dramatically. She toured all over the United States to increasing press coverage and larger audiences. She was a big hit in California and then in New York. Her big opportunity came when her manager arranged for her to perform in England in November 1891.

THE EXPULSION OF
HENRY E. KREUTZ

She performed twice on the voyage to England, despite being seasick most of the time. She must have dazzled the upper crust passengers, as within days of her arrival she was invited to Sandringham to perform for the Prince of Wales at his birthday party. She was a great hit with the future King of England and his influential guests. Her performances in London in the weeks that followed packed houses. The Alhambra, where she performed, held an audience of four thousand. People waited for hours for tickets. Newspapers were full of the remarkable and mysterious story of her powers. The British medical and scientific community was as mystified as had been those in America.

After London, she spent a year touring Europe. She performed in front of Emperor Franz Josef of Austria, Kaiser Wilhelm of Germany and the Czar of Russia, as well as other members of the royal families of Europe. She was extremely successful wherever she went. Her simple tricks combined with a lot of charisma and personal charm won over many important and well-educated people. She returned to the United States in 1893 and played once again at Milledgeville's Opera House.

Dixie Haygood never was to regain the glory that was hers during her British and European tour. She toured the United States extensively until about 1910, with brief interludes as housewife and even as a baker. Her managers used her and stole from her. Professionally, her act was imitated by imposters who used her name or a variation of it. These imposters, of dubious skill, obscured her identity to the point that the knowledge of who she was, where she was and what she had accomplished was lost. Despite others who imitated her work and imposters who attempted to take her identity, she was one of the most remarkable performers of her day.

Her personal life was a series of disasters. She was in and out of marriages and relationships. She never knew some of her children. Others she either turned her back on or they turned against her. Her son, Charles Jr., died as a teenager and is buried in an unmarked grave in Memory Hill.

In 1911, she gave her last performance at the Opera House, ending her career in the same building in which she had started more than a quarter of a century earlier. Her health was poor and declined until her death in 1915. She was buried in Memory Hill in an unmarked grave. In 2001, my wife Sue and I, along with some descendants, had a headstone placed on her grave. It reads, "Dixie Annie Jarratt Haygood, Died November 15, 1915, aged 54 years, also known as Annie Abbott 'the Little Georgia Magnet.'"

THE PROHIBITION QUESTION IN THE early spring of 1886 brought tremendous strife and friction to Baldwin County. Large numbers of the population were taking active and vocal sides in the debate. During a heated rally on Hancock Street on February 27, Deputy Marshal Charles N. Haygood was involved in a verbal confrontation with Elias N. "Sam" Ennis, which ended with Haygood being fatally shot. A few days later the city council banned public speaking in Milledgeville in an effort to curb violence.

Less than a month later, on Tuesday, March 23, bar owner Henry E. Kreutz was enthusiastically encouraging a huge demonstration of about fifteen hundred mostly black men and women attending an anti-Prohibition barbeque along the Oconee River. A procession of about a thousand marched through Milledgeville shouting slogans before returning to the banks of the river. Kreutz rode up and down the procession giving them liquor and encouraging them.

That evening, in his bar-room, Kreutz suggested that if any white ladies said anything about Prohibition, "insulting proposals" should be made to them.

The next morning, a citizens' committee visited Kreutz and told him that he must leave Baldwin County by 5:00 p.m. and that he was not to return. Kreutz argued that he had been drunk the day before but the committee was adamant. Within two hours, Kreutz headed out of town toward Toomsboro in a buggy.

Later that same day, a large gathering of citizens met to decide on a course of action. Dr. Iverson L. Harris was elected chairman and Lyman H. Compton, secretary. A committee of ten leading citizens was appointed to "draft suitable resolutions on the action of some of our citizens in giving notice to Henry Kreutz to leave the city." Harris appointed R.L. Hunter chairman; others on the committee were W.H. Scott, C.P. Crawford, Dr. W.H. Hall, T.T. Windsor, Jos. Staley, Dr. T.O. Powell, B.T. Bethune, F.B. Mapp and G.T. Whilden. The committee retired to discuss the assignment.

When they returned, they had several resolutions condemning the conduct of the marchers of the previous day, as well as anyone who encouraged them. Also, they added that, "H.E. Kreutz is manifestly guilty of aiding and abetting these disorders, by riding in line with them, furnishing them liquor, leading and cheering them through our streets, and counseling them to insolence towards our people and especially towards ladies, and whereas certain citizens have this morning warned said Kreutz to leave this county at once...we most cordially approve the action of those gentlemen, and adopt it as our own."

The resolutions were unanimously approved. Mr. B.T. Bethune moved that the meeting extend their sympathies to the family of Henry E. Kreutz and pledge themselves to protect and defend them against any danger that might arise whatever, while in Milledgeville. The motion was adopted. It was rumored that the citizens of Toomsboro warned Kreutz that he must keep moving or he would be lynched.

Some may say that the action by the committee in Milledgeville was very heavy handed and illegal. Others may take the point of view that these leading citizens of the 1880s were faced with the potential for large scale civil unrest that they had no way of controlling. The expulsion of Henry Kreutz, therefore, was a necessity in their efforts to defuse a very tense and dangerous situation.

MAJOR GENERAL
JOSEPH WARREN'S TEETH

REGRETTABLY, JOSEPH WARREN IS MOSTLY forgotten today. His participation in the American Revolution was important and intense. However, his untimely death caused him to be overshadowed by other longer lived Patriots who achieved fame. His teeth, however, if nothing else, raise him from the commonplace and into a realm where he should be remembered.

Joseph Warren was born near Boston in 1741. He graduated from Harvard in 1759 and became a well-known medical doctor in Boston. He was well acquainted with John and Sam Adams. He joined Sam Adams, John Hancock and James Otis as a political writer, speaker and organizer for the Patriot cause in pre–Revolutionary War Boston.

In 1775, he was the head of the Committee of Safety, which was the organization that controlled the Patriot resistance to the British occupation of Boston. In April of 1775, it was Joseph Warren who sent Paul Revere and William Dawes on their famed late-night rides to alarm the countryside of the Redcoat expedition to Lexington and Concord. As he was the leader of the "rebel" organization, he placed himself in great personal danger by staying in Boston when most of the Patriots had left and the British were on the lookout for "troublemakers."

Although he was not at Lexington or Concord, he did join in the fight against the Redcoats as they struggled back to Boston on April 19, 1775. On April 23, Warren succeeded John Hancock as president of the Massachusetts Provisional Congress. On May 20, he became the head of the committee to organize the army in Massachusetts. He declined the position of physician general and was elected major general of militia.

On the afternoon of June 17, 1775, Warren joined the Patriot forces at Bunker Hill. There, General Israel Putnam offered to turn over the command to him. He declined saying that he had been elected major general but his commission had not yet reached him; so he had rank only, but no command. Warren obtained a musket and ammunition from a retreating soldier and went to the exposed position called Breed's Hill where the Patriots had put up a dirt redoubt. He was wearing a light colored coat, wig and white fringed waistcoat.

Three successive waves of Redcoats, marching as on parade, came within "whites of their eyes" distance. The Redcoats faced a withering fire from Patriot muskets and took tremendous casualties. The third wave, however, overwhelmed the Patriot forces. Many fled, some stayed and fought until shot or bayoneted by the Redcoats. Joseph Warren was one of those who stayed, and died at the age of thirty-four.

Warren had been shot through the face at the redoubt. He died instantly. His clothes had been taken by a Redcoat soldier and sold in the streets of Boston. Warren's body was buried in the redoubt and then dug up again to be exhibited to onlookers, including General John Burgoyne who came across the river from Boston to view the remains. Warren was reburied in the redoubt in a grave along with the body of an unidentified Patriot soldier who was wearing a farmer's shirt.

Almost a year later, efforts were made to locate his body. Several British officers had described seeing Warren's body and gave a general idea of where it was buried. These officers now were aboard ships, as the British were forced by George Washington's forces to evacuate Boston in 1776.

Two brothers of Dr. Warren, a sexton, some friends and Paul Revere went to the old redoubt to try and locate the body. In what must have been an extremely grisly and disagreeable task they dug into the area that held a couple hundred hastily buried Patriots.

They discovered the unknown farmer's remains wearing the shirt. With it they found remains that they believed had been Warren. It was known that Warren had been shot in the face and this skeleton had been shot in the face. Paul Revere made the positive identification. He had made Warren a set of two false teeth about a year earlier. This skull had the two false teeth and Paul Revere was able to identify his own work.

Warren's remains were taken to the Old Granary Cemetery in Boston. Later, he was moved to Forest Hills Cemetery outside of Boston. Joseph Warren was an important leader and heroic Patriot who deserves to be remembered. In Milledgeville, we are reminded of him by Warren Street, which is named for him. There is also Warren County in Georgia named for him. We also can remember him as being the first person ever to be identified after death by dental records.

A Case of Bigamy

I N THE SUMMER OF 1871, Milledgeville was shocked and outraged as the charge of bigamy "destroyed the happiness of one of the best families in the state." In April, twenty-three-year-old Sallie Myrick, a niece of General Stith P. Myrick, had married a gentleman by the name of John T. Snead. Less than two months later, Snead was arrested and charged with bigamy.

Mr. Snead was married on May 31, 1861, to Anna H. Robbins in Liberty, Bedford County, Virginia. Snead lived with his wife Anna in various cities, including Charleston, Washington, D.C., New York and Boston until the summer of 1870. At that time he came to Georgia and was employed in Macon. His wife was left behind in New York.

Snead apparently was well liked in Milledgeville. He had been introduced to his future bride by General Myrick himself at the general's home. After Snead's arrest, he could not post the required bail of $2,000, so he was placed in the jail. The sheriff, Obadiah Arnold, allowed Snead the unusual option of hiring two "reliable men as guards" who would accompany Snead, and so freed him from prison until his trial.

The townspeople, after getting over the initial shock at the charges, tended to soften their feelings toward Snead and hoped that he would be able to clear up the record, not just for the sake of Sallie Myrick Snead and the Myrick family, but also for Snead himself.

The arrangement with the guards did not work out as the trial was not until August. Snead was put back into jail. Snead retained the firm of Crawford and Williams, as well as Colonel Simmons, for his defense. The prosecutors were the firm of Sanford and Furman, Colonel Briscoe and John B. Weems. The prosecution team brought Anna Snead to Milledgeville to testify against John Snead. In the course of their investigation, the prosecuting attorneys had learned that the manager of the hotel where the marriage had taken place, W.C. Hewitt, was now managing a hotel in Georgia. Hewitt had not only witnessed the 1861 marriage but had also personally brought the minister to the hotel to perform the marriage. The prosecutors went in search of Hewitt to subpoena him as a witness. He would be an independent witness and thus their case would be solid. However,

Hewitt was found to be too sick to travel to Milledgeville. Hewitt was willing to testify and wrote the judge a letter asking to be excused for the moment, but that, when he was well, he would come to Milledgeville to testify. One of the prosecutors, John H. Furman, brought this letter back to Milledgeville.

To his horror, Furman found that the other lawyers prosecuting the case did not believe that they needed Hewitt's testimony and were urging the judge to proceed with the trial. Furman, who had been on the case since the first arrest, pleaded with them to no avail. He only remained on the prosecution team because General Myrick urged him to stay.

Before the trial, it was suggested that Snead's defense would be that he actually had been married before his marriage to Anna Robbins and that his first wife had been alive when he married Robbins, and therefore his marriage to Robbins was unlawful. However, his first wife had since died and so he was free to marry Sallie Myrick.

The prosecution presented its case at the trial. Without Hewitt they could not produce an independent witness to the marriage with Anna Robbins. They produced letters where Snead referred to Robbins as his wife. They also produced witnesses who had met Anna Robbins in New York and had been introduced to her as Mrs. Snead, wife of John T. Snead.

The defense team offered no defense at all. When the judge charged the jury he made it clear that he thought Snead was guilty. The jurors were Charles E. Bonner, Thomas Prosser, W.H. Torrence, M.W. Ethridge, R.D. Ivey, M.A. Barnes, J.M. Nosworthy, H.E. Hendrix, H. Perry, E.H. Walls, John Jones and Mansfield Jenkins. They acquitted John Snead.

The newspaper was not kind to Mr. Snead. They printed a long open letter from prosecutor Furman, who gave, in minute detail, the life of Snead, his marriage to Anna Robbins and their various employments and residences. Furman also strongly condemned the attorneys who went forward with the case knowing that their principle witness was not available.

He saved his strongest comments for the jury and for Snead. He began by saying,

When society has been outraged—when a black-hearted villain has been turned loose to again satiate his hell-born lusts in the bosom of some unsuspecting community, all good men stand wondering and astonished. So it is with the bigamy case that has just been decided by what is called an intelligent jury for Baldwin County.

Immediately after the trial, Snead left for parts unknown. Furman wrote that, "I sincerely hope that should [Snead] again turn up in any community within the borders of this State justice shall be meted out to him."

The *Southern Recorder* said the case "should be a warning to Southern young ladies, to receive, with great caution, the attentions of strangers from the North, or elsewhere, of whose antecedents they know nothing, and may not discover, as in [this] instance, until it is too late."

Sallie Myrick died in 1903 and is buried in Memory Hill Cemetery. She never married again.

The Mysterious Duel of
James Spalding

THE NAME JAMES SPALDING ISN'T well known in central Georgia. In fact, I don't think he is known at all. He is one of the state legislators buried on the west side of Memory Hill Cemetery. He, along with the others, died in Milledgeville when the legislature was in session and, as transportation was difficult at that time, was buried here. Because these men represented counties other than our own, they have been ignored.

James Spalding, the representative of McIntosh County, died Friday, November 24, 1820. He was three weeks shy of his twenty-third birthday. The tombstone over his grave was authorized by the Georgia General Assembly five years later.

The tombstone reads:

Sacred to the memory of James Spalding, Esq., son of Thomas Spalding, who whilst representing the county of McIntosh in the Legislature, died at Milledgeville 24th Nov. 1820 in the 23rd year of his age. Lamented by his friends for his many virtues and regretted by all for the prematurity of his fate. His earlier life had been devoted to the service of the Navy, under three gallant commanders, [Stephen] Decatur, [Jacob] Jones and [Lewis] Warrington. To a fine genius he united a cultivated understanding and to an elevated patriotism a delicate sense of honor, giving promise of much usefulness to his country.

"A delicate sense of honor" may be interpreted as an indication that the writer of the epitaph knew something, that we, 180 years later, do not.

Perhaps curiously, Charles Mathews, a state senator, died Wednesday, November 22, 1820, two days before James Spalding. Mathews was from Morgan County and his body was taken there for burial. His grave has not been located so we have no knowledge of what may have been inscribed on his tombstone. There is no record of the state providing him with a marker as was done for Spalding.

Spalding's tombstone mentions that Spalding served in the navy. In fact, he served for five years. He was commissioned as a midshipman November 9, 1813, at the age of fifteen. He served aboard several ships in the Mediterranean and saw action against the Barbary pirates. One of his commanders, Stephen Decatur, was a dashing officer who had gained a reputation for audacity and bravery and who had been involved in several duels. In fact, Decatur was killed in a duel in March of 1820. When Spalding left the navy, about 1818, he went into politics and was elected as the state representative from McIntosh County. He was re-elected in 1820.

The *Southern Recorder* said, "A melancholy occurrence, such as has not before happened within our recollection during any session of the General Assembly, the death of two members of the Legislative Body, took place last week—both of them victims to the *disease of the season* which is so common throughout the country." One might look at the phrase "*disease of the season*" and suspect it pointed to something unusual. However, the *Georgia Journal* made a similar sentiment: "[Spalding] was suddenly seized with the prevailing epidemic (influenza) and fell a victim to its violence on the 13th day of its attack." This sounds far less like something sinister had taken place.

The reports by the Senate regarding Mathews, and the House of Representatives regarding Spalding, do not give any hints that anything was amiss other than premature and unexpected deaths. They are typical of the obituaries and expressions of mourning for the period.

James Spalding was the son of Thomas and Sarah Spalding of St. Simons Island. Sarah kept a "Book of the Dead" where she recorded her grief. When James died, Sarah wrote a long paragraph about him:

Noble and impetuous, he could not brook control, because conscious that no sinister motive ever swayed him. Whenever he met vice unmasked, it met his undissembled scorn, however dignified by wealth or power; but who so liable to be deceived as the generous and the good, suspicion does not darken the untainted mind until bitter experience has made us acquainted with the Protens [Latin, means "extension"], vice—A monster claimed his friendship, he believed him like himself—A tale of varnished falsehood, oppression, wrong (but hidden guilt) drew his sympathy—In Honors cause, as he believed, he became his champion, ventured his life, and in what is deemed among Men, honorable contest, slew his adversary: Oh God of Mercy, blot out the remembrance of this sin, and let the unavailing regret, the bitter remorse, the never dying sensibility of a mind rich in worth, teach this solemn lesson, that at the touch of Evil, all that beautifies Mortality crumbles into dust—Honor, Intellect, Virtue, but contributed to sap the foundation of life, and give a Grave in manhood's early bloom to him we mourn. The frail tenement of clay is dissolved, but the imprisoned Spirit set free by its tried companion's fall, I trust is expatiating in regions of Bliss on the riches of Eternity. Where the assembled universe shall meet, may I see thee, my Son, an adoring Seraph at the feet of Jesus, rapt in the contemplation of Redeeming love.

No evidence of a duel has ever been uncovered. However, from Sarah Spalding's outpouring there can be little doubt that she refers to a duel when she says, "in what is deemed among Men, honorable contest, slew his adversary." It is apparent that Spalding met a "monster" and that Spalding "became [the monster's] champion." After the successful duel Spalding experienced "unavailing regret, the bitter remorse" of his actions.

There is no evidence that Spalding's opponent was Charles Mathews, other than the close proximity of their deaths. The duel may well have taken place weeks, months or perhaps years before. But, a duel there was. However, it seems unlikely we will ever learn more about it than what we know now.

THE HARRIS-
SANFORD MURDER

MURDERS ARE ALWAYS TO SOME degree disagreeable. Some may be interesting, even fascinating, but there is always something disagreeable about a cold-blooded killing. This is particularly true when the perpetrator and victim are both children. That is what happened in Milledgeville in 1841. William "Bill" A. Harris, the fourteen-year-old son of the prominent lawyer Iverson L. Harris, stabbed to death Richard H. Sanford, the twelve-year-old son of General John W.A. Sanford.

The local newspapers did not cover the crime nor the trial. I would suspect that the powerful and influential fathers of these boys kept the story out of the papers. I am surprised, however, that other papers did not pick up the story. The only surviving evidence relating to the murder are some letters by young Sanford's grandfather, the Reverend Richard M. Blount, and a few remarks by Judge Iverson L. Harris in his autobiography.

The boys were students at Oglethorpe University in Midway. On Sunday, June 27, 1841, they were playing at a creek. For some unknown reason, the young Harris boy urinated on Sanford. Harris was carrying a stick and a pistol, so Sanford did not retaliate in any way. The following day during recess at school, Harris borrowed a knife and whetted the longest blade. When the owner of the knife asked for it back, Harris refused, saying that he had a use for it. Harris then went in search of Sanford.

Richard Sanford was in an upstairs room reading when he was approached by Harris. Harris tried to pick a fight with Sanford. Seeing that Harris was armed with both a pistol and a knife, Sanford told Harris that if Harris would lay aside his weapons he, Sanford, would fight him with his fists. At this time Harris was sitting on a bench to the left side of Sanford. Holding the knife in his right hand, Harris struck Sanford backhanded, driving the knife into the right side of Sanford's chest. A second stab with the knife struck Sanford's hand and the third his wrist as he was trying to defend himself. At this time the attack was broken up by another student, thirteen-year-old Leonidas Jordan.

Sanford clung to life for ten days, then died. At a postmortem examination, it was determined that the knife had passed between the third and fourth ribs, cut an artery and pierced the membrane that covers the right lobe of the lung. Harris was arrested and charged with murder.

Iverson Harris said that he was offered assistance in the defense of his son by a number of lawyers. He accepted Judge Berrien, Judge Joseph Lumpkin and Judge Cone as the defense team. The trial was to be in November.

The lawyers prosecuting the case were General Augustus Reese, Judge Walter T. Colquitt and F.H. Sanford. It is interesting that Iverson Harris said that "Judge Colquitt was evidently not in his right element. He felt it. It emasculated his powers. Privately he spoke of it. He had been urged and entreated by many of his warm friends, ladies and gentlemen, to withdraw from the case, and doubtless he would have done so, but he was overcome by temptation of a large fee."

The trial was short. The deliberations of the jury were even shorter. After three minutes, the jury came back with a verdict: not guilty. Reverend Blount was outraged. He wrote to a friend, "a large majority of the bar seems to stick together as close as a gang of bandits, to screen a culprit from the rope—and why? Because he was a lawyer's son." He continues, "I shall hereafter consider a large majority of them as a dangerous part of the community and opposed to equal justice. I would never go to a class of men, who could be hired to do wrong," and "they volunteer to save each other."

After the trial, Iverson Harris must have thought it would be best if his son left town. He was enrolled in a school in Granville, Massachusetts, and later Vermont. During the Mexican War, he served in the United States Army with the Macon Guards, First Regiment, Georgia Volunteers. Returning to Milledgeville after the war, he read law in his father's law office. After being admitted to the bar, he moved to Irwin County to open his practice. Soon, Worth County was formed and he established his practice there. During the Civil War, he enlisted in the Fourteenth Georgia Infantry where he became a lieutenant colonel.

Harris was elected to the Senate from Worth County in 1859 and 1860. After the war, he returned to his law practice. He was reelected to the Senate in 1873 and became known as "Bill Harris of Worth." For almost twenty years, he was secretary of the Georgia Senate.

Harris died August 17, 1894, at the age of sixty-seven at his home in Worth County. His body was brought to Milledgeville by train to be buried in Memory Hill Cemetery in the lot with his ancestors. The train arrived so late in the day that it was nearly dark when the casket was lowered into the ground. The minister had to read the burial service by lantern light. It was growing too late for the Masons' ceremony, so the worshipful master, R.W. Roberts, simply placed a white apron and glove in the grave.

The funeral of young Richard Sanford was not recorded by the newspapers. The location of his grave, even which cemetery it is in, has been lost. Lost, too, has been the story of this senseless tragedy.

THE STATE HOUSE FIRE OF 1833

THE STATE HOUSE, OR AS it is called now the Old Capitol Building, has survived several fires. In fact, this amazing building has been destroyed several times. Like a phoenix, it rises from its ashes. The fire of 1894 consumed the building, but the state rebuilt it. The reconstructed building was again virtually destroyed in the 1940s. After the reconstruction, the building was called the "New Administration Building" by Georgia Military College.

Of particular interest, however, is the State House fire of 1833. It did not destroy the building, but it was a near thing. Despite it being so far in the past, we are fortunate in having several eyewitnesses who have left us with vivid descriptions.

The fire started about noon on November 16, 1833. It was first noticed burning on the roof of the State House just to the north of the cupola. Both houses of the legislature had just adjourned; there were many legislators and employees of the state on and in the premises.

Large numbers of the public literally ran to the scene of the fire to help. People came from all over town. Ladies were seen running with buckets and pitchers of water. Men carried water, blankets and carpets to aid in smothering the flames. It was mentioned in the newspapers of the day that many blacks, not waiting for instructions from their masters, rushed to the scene and actively worked side by side with whites in the fight to save the building.

It was apparent from the first that the building was in grave danger. Most thought that it could not be saved. Many people busied themselves carrying furniture out of the building to the safety of the grounds. Offices and the library were quickly emptied. State papers, records and books were all brought out and left on the grass as the people ran back for more. The Bank of Georgia and the state treasury were particular problems, as they contained not only records but large stacks of cash and bonds. The public carried armloads of cash outside. Within an hour, the State House was empty of valuables.

Getting water to the fire presented a considerable challenge. Wells were at remote locations and the building was very high. Buckets of water were passed by a line of people from the wells into the State House, and up the two flights of stairs and then handed through holes in the ceilings or continued on up the stairs to the cupola where they were passed to men on the roof. Hundreds of people were involved in the effort.

The fire on the roof was being fanned by a strong wind from the northwest. The roof being both high and steep made fighting the fire very difficult. The State House did not own a fire engine of any kind. The city had one that came to the scene, but it did not have the power to spray water beyond the eaves of the building. There were no ladders long enough to reach the eaves.

A black man by the name of Big Sam, belonging to the architect and builder John Marlor, was conspicuous in his courageous work on the roof. He was among the first to get on the roof and fought the fire from there. When roof shingles began to burn near the eaves he would walk down the steep, wet roof and remove them, tossing them to the ground. He did this without a safety rope of any kind. Quite a crowd assembled below watching him with "agonized solicitude" as he did what no other man dared attempt.

Other men singled out for their meritorious services during the fire were Senator Dunnagan from Hall County, Representative McElvoy from Decatur, Representative Young from Irwin, Senator Stapleton from Jefferson, Senator Fields from Lumpkin, A.H. Pemberton of Augusta, Peter J. Williams and John Marlor of Milledgeville and Solomon Smith of Montgomery, Alabama, the manager of the theater. The *Georgia Journal* went so far as to say the State House would not have been saved without these men.

Big Sam was singled out for special mention among these heroes of the fire. The *Georgia Journal* suggested that he be "signally rewarded by the Legislature in mere justice to his bravery and zeal." The *Federal Union* took that recommendation a step further by saying Big Sam "gallantly hazarded his life to save the Capital, and the representatives of the people should reward his extraordinary zeal in the service of the State, by bestowing freedom on him."

The legislature did vote $1,800 for the purchase of Big Sam from John Marlor with the intention of giving him his freedom. However, they neglected to pass an act for his emancipation. For the next nineteen years, Big Sam worked around the State House doing maintenance, as he was legally the property of the state. In 1852, the governor urged the legislature to pass the required act and Big Sam was given his freedom.

The fire was believed to have started on the roof from sparks from one of the chimneys. The roof was made of pine shingles and easily combustible. A year later, the roof was covered with copper to make it safe from fire.

After the fire a guard was assigned to protect the money lying on the State House grounds. There was no report of anyone taking the opportunity to steal anything. Many people worked into the evening, and on Sunday continued gathering up the books, furniture, records and documents to return them to the State House. Despite the fire, the water damage and the disarranged papers, both branches of the legislature transacted business as usual on Monday.

The fire of 1833 is remarkable in that the citizenry so quickly, and in such numbers, came to the aid of the structure. Their successful fight to save a public building and contents is a display of civic spirit that is rare today.

Husband Illegally
Puts His Wife in Asylum

THE IDEA OF HAVING TO put a loved one into a mental hospital is awful to contemplate. However, it is far worse when a loved one forces a mentally healthy spouse into a mental hospital. That is what happened to Adele Louise Tucker.

Adele Louise Tucker was born October 28, 1882. In the early 1900s, she was a militant suffragette and was active in politics until 1930. She became a very prosperous businesswoman in Jacksonville, Florida. She made a considerable fortune in real estate.

In the late 1920s her husband, William Henry Tucker, made false allegations about her sanity. It is presumed that his motive was to take control of her assets and get her out of the way. On March 15, 1930, at the age of forty-seven, Adele Louise Tucker was admitted to the state mental hospital in Milledgeville.

One can only imagine the horror experienced by a sane person who is wrongfully incarcerated in a mental hospital. Protesting her sanity would be to no avail. Mrs. Tucker began a campaign to regain her freedom. No doubt she also wanted revenge on her husband and to regain her stolen assets.

While she was in the hospital, a dummy corporation was set up that dispersed her wealth. Many individuals and companies were involved. Year after year passed with Mrs. Tucker still being held against her will in the mental hospital. After twelve years her husband died. She could no longer hope to get her revenge on him. But she kept on fighting for her freedom.

On June 18, 1947, after seventeen years and three months of confinement, which must have seemed an eternity, she was released from the hospital. She was now sixty-four years old. Her legal battles continued as she fought to regain what she could of her lost wealth. She filed lawsuits against the people who were alleged to be her guardians as well as companies that acquired her assets. She was partially successful in reclaiming what had been hers before her commitment to the hospital.

After her release, Mrs. Tucker worked as a cashier in a dry cleaning plant. The superintendent of the state hospital allowed Mrs. Tucker to move into a mobile home on state property. In March 1976, at the age of ninety-three, she was still living there. At that time, the General Assembly of Georgia transferred to Mrs. Tucker a life estate in the property where she lived. After her death, the land where she lived was to revert to state ownership and would be named "Adele Louise Tucker Park."

Patients in mental institutions have been known to say, "before you lock us up, take a good look at those who bring us in." No doubt Mrs. Tucker would heartily agree with that sentiment. Mrs. Tucker died in January 1983, at the age of one hundred.

Treating a Scalped Head

IN THE EARLY DAYS OF the settlement of Georgia and other states, there were numerous conflicts between the settlers and the Indians. This area of confrontation moved with the frontiers, generally westward, as the Indians were forced to give up more and more of their land. Often the frontiers were the scenes of attacks, ambushes or raids, and these were frequently followed by retaliatory attacks.

Part of this violence involved the taking of scalps. Scalps often were regarded as trophies of battle and of conquest by the Indians. Whites, too, would scalp their slain Indian enemies. Sometimes whites would pay a bounty on Indian scalps as proof that an Indian had been killed.

We usually think of scalping as something that was done to a dead enemy's body. This was not always the case. Sometimes the victim did not die from their wounds and other times the scalping victim may not have been wounded prior to being scalped. The problem arose as to what medical treatment was appropriate for a scalped head.

Survivors of scalping were not as rare as one might think. Unfortunately, there were quite a few people who experienced this horror. There was a woman, "Old Mrs. Clarke" in Milledgeville in 1827, who had been scalped. She had a silver plate "in her skull" covering the exposed bone. This apparently had been successful but it was not the treatment of choice.

Exposed bone would eventually become necrotic and separate from the healthy bone. It may also cause osteomyelitis, an inflammation of the bone and marrow. Either of these situations would likely be fatal. The bone must be covered and blood flow established.

A shadowy figure by the name of Dr. Patrick Vance or Kilpatrick Vance successfully treated scalping victims on the American frontier in the late 1700s. It was he who taught the far better known James Robertson the technique. Robertson was not a doctor. He was a pioneer best known as the founder of Nashville and the "father of Tennessee." Robertson's son, Felix, was a medical doctor who recorded his father's experiences in an 1806 article called "Remarks on the Management of a Scalped-Head." Dr. Felix Robertson describes how Dr. Vance taught James Robertson how to treat a scalp wound. Trained medical doctors were scarce on the frontiers and often medical procedures were, by necessity, performed by laymen.

James Robertson's first experience with a scalping victim was in 1777. One Frederick Calvit was scalped with "nearly the whole of his head skinned." He was being treated by Dr. Vance. However, Vance could not stay with his patient during the whole course of the treatment, so he instructed James Robertson in the art of skull boring. Robertson was directed to "bore the skull as it got black," and "he bored a few holes himself, to show the manner of doing it."

Robertson continued, "I have found that a flat pointed straight awl is the best instrument to bore with, as the skull is thick, and somewhat difficult to penetrate. When the awl is nearly through, this instrument should be borne more lightly upon. The time to quit boring is when a reddish fluid appears on the point of the awl. I bore, at first, about one inch apart, and, as the flesh appears to rise in those holes, I bore a number more between the first." Frederick Calvit recovered from his injuries.

The idea is that through these small holes "fleshy projections form on the surface of a gaping wound." These granulations produce a growth of new capillaries and scar tissue, or "proud-flesh," which provides the area with a blood supply. After boring, the wound had to be kept clean and dressed daily to prevent infection.

The success rate for the treatment was apparently quite good. It did take a long time, however. The average recovery period was two years. Robertson reported that hair would also grow back on the new scalp although not as thickly as on the original scalp. The boring process apparently was not painful. The patient would regain feeling once the new scalp grew enough to attach to the edge of the uninjured part of the scalp.

This same boring treatment was used, and still is used, to treat other scalping type injuries. For example, women would sometimes get their hair caught in machinery during the Industrial Revolution. Whenever bare bone was exposed, the boring method has been used. The treatment also works well with burn victims.

In 1849, Milledgeville's famous Dr. Tomlinson Fort wrote a book entitled *Dissertation on the Practice of Medicine*, which describes many of the treatments used at that time. I don't believe that he ever treated a scalped head. However, he was a greatly experienced practitioner and likely knew of James Robertson's treatment.

NEVER PULL AN ARROW
OUT OF A BODY

ROUGHLY TWO HUNDRED YEARS AGO, the western frontier ran through Georgia. The white settlers to the east were continually pressured to move west into new lands. Through various schemes including treaties, forced treaties and outright warfare, the Indians were pushed to the west. This was a time of great conflict between the two cultures. Raids, ambushes and retaliatory attacks, by both sides, were frequent.

The settlers and soldiers were armed with firearms. The Indians were armed with bows and arrows as well as the occasional firearm. Firearms created problems for the Indians, however, in that they required ammunition, maintenance and spare parts. Firearms were sometimes traded to the Indians, but the Indians' primary source for them and the additional items needed to keep them shooting was by theft from whites or taking them from those killed in battle. Bows and arrows, however, were a renewable resource.

We've all watched movies where an arrow sinks deep into the body of a man who drops to the ground in pain but rarely in agony. Twentieth-century moviegoers have seen countless arrows yanked out of victims, the wound bandaged and the man back in the fight. The reality of life on the frontier was much different and far more gruesome, and the treatment of the arrow wound far more complex, excruciatingly painful and dangerous than Hollywood has led us to believe.

Arrows produced injuries that required special treatment methods. There is very little medical or historical information on the wounds made by arrows. The principle work on the subject is Dr. Joseph Howland Bill's twenty-two-page article "Notes on Arrow Wounds," which appeared in the *American Journal of Medical Sciences* in 1862. Dr. Bill was a lieutenant in the U.S. Army stationed at Fort Defiance, New Mexico in 1860. While there he observed and treated many arrow wounds. It may be inferred that the treatment practiced and described by Dr. Bill was essentially similar to that used in earlier times and places on the frontier.

When the Indian craftsman was assembling the arrow, the arrowhead was tied on using animal tendons and sinews. This kept the arrowhead secure, until the fastening material got wet with blood or other bodily fluids. Once wet, the arrowhead would become loose and easily separate from the shaft. Dr. Bill explained that the worst thing a friend could do was to try to remove the arrow by pulling on the shaft. It was very likely that the arrowhead would be left behind, forcing the doctor to search for it.

Searching for an arrowhead lost in a body could be nasty indeed. If the arrowhead was still attached to the shaft, the physician would make an incision to enlarge the entry wound and slide a finger down the shaft to feel the depth of the wound. It is also necessary to determine if the arrowhead is stuck into bone. If the shaft had been removed, leaving the arrowhead behind, the doctor is forced to dig through tissue in an attempt to find the arrowhead. This causes a great deal more trauma. There is, of course, the grave danger that the arrowhead could not be located. If the arrowhead is left behind, the patient is certain to die.

Once the doctor has located the arrowhead, either still attached to the shaft or separately, it can be removed with forceps or by putting a wire loop around it. Removing the shaft and arrowhead together is the ideal method. When the arrowhead is stuck into bone, the force necessary to dislodge it can be enough to bend forceps.

Wounds to arms—which were common, as soldiers often tried to shield themselves with raised hands and arms—would usually show a "small and narrow slit" with reddish bruising at the entrance wound. The exit wound would be larger but without the bruise. As long as this type of wound did not get infected, recovery was excellent.

Wounds to the trunk were far more difficult. If the spine was hit, the wound would likely be fatal. Of the fifteen men Dr. Bill saw with chest wounds, six had injured lungs and four of them died. All nine of the men examined without injuries to the lungs survived.

Abdominal wounds were exceedingly dangerous. Of the twenty-one abdominal wound cases Dr. Bill examined, all but one died. The likelihood of an infection from a punctured intestine was very high. Dr. Bill would enlarge abdominal wounds in order that he could examine the abdominal cavity. He used gold wire to suture lacerated intestines. However, the results were discouraging.

The most important things to remember from Dr. Bill's study of arrow wounds is that that wounds to the abdomen are usually fatal, an arrowhead left in a patient was fatal and that yanking an arrow shaft out of the body often resulted in the arrowhead being left in the wound, causing additional complications.

While these instructions are of little use to us today, they were undoubtedly widely known in the past. The next time a movie shows a man pulling an arrow out of his buddy's body, keep in mind that it's not an approved technique.

George Washington's First Crisis
as Commanding General

In central Georgia there are many places named for George Washington. In Milledgeville, Washington Street leads west from the old State House square. In other chapters, I have used the streets of Milledgeville named for famous Revolutionary War characters as a pretense for writing about the lives of these men. Perhaps the best way to describe what Washington did during the American Revolution is to say that when "the buck stops here," the buck was in Washington's lap. He carried the burden of the Revolution continuously from start to finish, something none of the other Founding Fathers did.

Washington's life cannot be condensed into a few pages and hoped to bring out anything that the reader doesn't already know. As an alternative, the following tale about Washington's first crisis in the Revolutionary War is one that is virtually unknown. The crisis however, was real, and if his handling had gone awry, the war for independence could have been won by the British in a single overwhelming victory.

Washington, sitting in his office in Cambridge, Massachusetts, sucked in his breath sharply as he read a letter that had been delivered by hand only moments before. It was dated August 1, 1775, from Elbridge Gerry, the chairman of the Committee of Supply of the Massachusetts Provincial Congress. To Washington's "very great astonishment," the supply of gunpowder for the Patriot army besieging Boston was 36 barrels. Washington had thought there were 308 barrels of gunpowder. Gerry went on to say that there were no flints for the muskets and only two tons of lead for bullets.

Washington thought of his army. This army was supposed to deal with the British in Boston just a few miles away. He had arrived in Cambridge on July 2, 1775, to take command of this army, "a mixed multitude of people here, under very little discipline, order, or government…confusion and disorder reigned in every department." One of the problems was that the army had materialized quickly after the Lexington/Concord fights of April and had taken up positions along a ten-mile crescent around Boston and the tip of the Charleston peninsula across the Charles River from Boston. He was bringing organization to the multitude of inexperienced officers and men. Now he was faced with his first major crisis.

Three major factors had to be addressed immediately. First, he needed to obtain more gunpowder as quickly as possible. Second, it was absolutely essential that the gunpowder shortage not become known to the British. To keep the shortage a secret, as few of his own people as possible should know of it. A word leaked to the British would surely bring on an immediate attack. It would be an attack that he could not possibly repulse. Washington had just under fourteen thousand men fit for duty. The vast majority of these men had never heard a shot fired in anger. The gunpowder crisis left his army with "not more than 9 cartridges a Man." This amateur army would be faced with over six thousand highly trained British regulars who carried sixty rounds per man, and had stockpiles to re-supply them as they used their ammunition. The British attack would be backed with artillery and heavy cannon fire from warships in the harbor. Clearly then, the third factor was that the British must be discouraged from making an attack.

Washington called a Council of War on August 3. He explained to his generals the critical need for gunpowder. The explanation for the discrepancy of what had been listed as being in store and what actually was available tells much about the inexperience of the American forces. The Committee of Supplies, "not being sufficiently acquainted with the nature of a return . . . sent in an account of all the ammunition which had been collected by the Province, so that the report included not only what was on hand but what had been spent." Therefore, 308 barrels had been collected and reported. The fact that all but 36 had been spent was left unsaid.

Besides seeking gunpowder from the provinces, other sources must be found for gunpowder. The Council of War agreed "by a great majority" to send a detachment of three hundred men to make an attempt to capture the British powder magazine at Halifax, Nova Scotia.

On August 4, Washington wrote to Governor Nicholas Cooke of Rhode Island for powder. He informed Cooke that "our necessities in the articles of powder and lead are so great as to require an immediate supply . . . forward every pound of each in the colony which can possibly be spared . . . no quantity, however small, is beneath notice and should any arrive I beg it may be forwarded as soon as possible." Washington then proposed that an armed ship be sent from Rhode Island and make an attempt to capture a powder magazine on Bermuda.

In his letter to the Committee of Safety of New Hampshire on August 4, 1775, Washington also begged for gunpowder saying, "the smallest quantities are not beneath notice . . . lead and flints are also very scarce . . . every hour in our present situation is critical."

Governor Jonathan Trumbull of Connecticut received a plea "in strict confidence" for "every ounce [of gunpowder] in the Province." Washington added that "the case calls loudly for the warmest and most strenuous exertions of every friend to his country, and does not admit of the least delay; no quantity however small is beneath notice."

A rumor was leaked to the British that the Patriots had eighteen hundred barrels of gunpowder. Washington also caused a rumor to be circulated in his own camp that he had so much gunpowder he was somewhat embarrassed by having so much.

Six weeks earlier, on June 14, 1775, the Continental Congress authorized the raising of rifle companies in Pennsylvania, Virginia and Maryland. Immediately, hundreds of young men from the western counties came forward to volunteer. These hardy men from the frontier used their rifles to bring in food and provide defense against Indians. As soon as they were organized, rifle companies marched to the aid of Boston. These riflemen would play a significant part in Washington's plans to survive until an adequate supply of gunpowder was at hand.

At that time, rifles were seen in the backwoods of Pennsylvania, Virginia and Maryland, as well as the Southern colonies, but in New England they were a novelty. Until the first rifle companies arrived, there were no rifles or riflemen on either side at the siege of Boston. The weapons used were smoothbores, which were not very accurate and had an effective range of fifty to seventy yards. Military training did not usually include marksmanship. The muskets did not even have rear sights. The muskets were much like 12-gauge shotguns. Soldiers were drilled in quick loading and firing on command when their weapons were "leveled" at the enemy. In the linear formations in use at the time, this was an effective method of delivering large numbers of balls in the general direction of the enemy. Volleys of musket fire were followed up with a bayonet charge. Rifles were new, hi-tech and terrifying to those who did not have them.

Washington, having been a colonel in the Virginia militia and having served actively in the French & Indian War, was well acquainted with the rifle and the men who used them. He looked forward to the arrival of the rifle companies. On July 18 , the first rifle company reached Cambridge from Berks County, Pennsylvania. Others soon followed. The riflemen went out of their way to cover ground quickly as well as to put on demonstrations of their marksmanship ability on their march to Massachusetts. Daniel Morgan marched his men 600 miles in twenty-one days, while Michael Cresap's company covered 550 miles in twenty-two days.

Most of the population was unfamiliar with the rifle. Striking a mark at distances two or three times as far as a smoothbore musket provoked awe in the onlookers. Word of this new and deadly capability spread quickly by word of mouth, letters and newspapers. The news carried to England as well. The shortcomings of the rifle—slow loading, quick to foul, non-standard ball size and no bayonet—were not recognized at this time. For now the only thing that was touted was the ability, often grossly exaggerated, of increasing the effective range of a weapon from "whites of their eyes" distance to several hundred yards.

The riflemen themselves also took on a mystical quality. Congressman Richard Henry Lee claimed that six counties in western Virginia could provide six thousand riflemen with "their amazing hardihood, their method of living so long in the woods without carrying provisions with them, the exceeding quickness with which they can march to distant parts, and above all, their dexterity . . . in the use of the Rifle Gun . . . every shot is fatal." Lee went so far as to assert that these riflemen could hit an orange at two hundred yards.

An eyewitness in Cambridge, Dr. James Thacher, described the riflemen as "remarkably stout and hardy men, many of them exceeding six feet in height. They are dressed in white frocks, or rifle-shirts, and round hats. These men are remarkable for the accuracy of their aim, striking a mark with great certainty at two hundred yards distance."

A "letter to a gentleman in Philadelphia" dated Fredericktown, Maryland, August 1, 1775, printed in several newspapers, gives us a glimpse of the impression the riflemen made on the general population. It also is a look at the riflemen themselves.

I have had the happiness of seeing Captain Michael Cresap marching at the head of a formidable company of upwards of one hundred and thirty men, from the mountains and back-woods, painted like Indians, armed with tomahawks and rifles, dressed in hunting-shirts and moccasins, and though some of them had traveled near eight hundred miles, from the banks of the Ohio, they seemed to walk light and easy, and not with less spirit than at the first hour of their march. Health and vigour, after what they had undergone, declared them to be intimate with hardship and familiar with danger.

The letter goes on to describe the riflemen's "dexterity at shooting."

A clapboard, with a mark the size of a dollar, was put up; they began to fire off-hand, and the bystanders were surprised, few shots being made that were not close to or in the paper. When they had shot for a time in this way, some lay on their backs, some on their breast or side, others ran twenty or thirty steps, and firing, appeared to be equally certain of the mark...One of the men took the board, and placing it between his legs, stood with his back to the tree while another drove the center. What would a regular army of considerable strength in the forest of America do with one thousand of these men, who want nothing to preserve their health and courage but water from the spring, with a little parched corn, with what they can easily procure in hunting; and who, wrapped in their blankets, in the damp of night, would choose the shade of a tree for their covering, and the earth for their bed.

On August 9, these riflemen arrived in Cambridge and placed themselves under the command of General Washington.

It was common practice for newspapers to pick up news items from other newspapers as well as to reprint letters, such as the one to the gentleman in Philadelphia. Thus, stories would rapidly spread far and wide. The *Virginia Gazette* of July 25, 1775, carried an article claiming that so many riflemen had volunteered for the rifle companies that a shooting test was required to weed down the numbers. It was claimed that the judges chalked a drawing of a human nose on a board and sixty men were said to have riddled the mark from 150 yards away. Such stories only added to the prestige and stature of the men in the hunting shirts. Like all tall tales they had a way of growing with each retelling, too.

To Washington, who desperately needed to keep the British from attacking during the ammunition crisis, the arrival of the riflemen was like an answer to a prayer. They brought with them not only their rifles but their fierce reputation as fighting men. This public fascination with the riflemen was far out of proportion to their actual usefulness, but for the short term they were just what was needed in this crisis. As soon as they arrived, they began to pick off British sentries and officers at great distance. The numbers of men killed by the riflemen was of little significance, but the terror factor and effect on morale was enormous. The British quickly learned the effective range of the rifle and gave the marksmen few targets. But the threat from the riflemen was always present.

The real value of the riflemen was to buy time for the Patriots. Washington seized the temporary excitement caused by the riflemen and worked it to his advantage. The riflemen were treated as privileged units. A few times the riflemen were used to creep out and attack small parties of British. Putting the fear of riflemen crawling about in the dark into the minds of the British would be one more idea to bother the enemy and keep them from contemplating an attack on the weak Patriot positions. However, Washington didn't want to use the riflemen frequently or the British would soon discover the weaknesses of the rifle in combat. Far better for the British to fear the unknown.

To make sure that the message was loud and clear Washington ordered a spectacular demonstration of the abilities of his riflemen. With a huge crowd of spectators on hand, Washington publicly had his men fire at a seven-inch diameter pole from 200 yards. The riflemen riddled the pole. Others fired at 250 yards. By the middle of August there were fourteen hundred riflemen facing the British in Boston. With their hunting shirts, they stood out from the mass of soldiers as an elite force.

Such marksmanship demonstrations and the loss of British soldiers exposed to their fire created discontent among the British in Boston and in England. General Howe wrote to England about "the terrible guns of the rebels." He was so concerned about the riflemen that he gave orders that one be taken prisoner along with his rifle. As soon as this was accomplished he had the rifleman sent to England to be exhibited.

By the end of August, the gunpowder crisis had eased. On August 24, Washington had 184 barrels of gunpowder as well as thousands of flints and several tons of lead. Throughout the war, supplies were never what were wanted but at least the men could have some ammunition in their cartridge boxes, as well as gunpowder stocks in store. The army, the public and the British never knew there had been a crisis. With the end of the gunpowder crisis, the riflemen, after having played such a major part in containing the British within Boston, became just another part of the Continental army.

The usefulness of the riflemen at Boston was over but they, without ever knowing it, had served a vital function. Without the intimidation of the riflemen, the British might easily have poured out of Boston, like fire ants boiling out of a mound, and put a sudden end to the fledgling Revolution. It would have been the end of George Washington, too.

INDEX

A

Abbott, Annie 78, 128, 129, 130
Adams, John 133
Adams, Sam 133
Allaman, James 52
Allen, J.T. 128
Allen, Mrs. H.D. 85
Ames, C.T. 53
Anna, General Santa 94
Anton, J. 115, 116
Archer, Jimmy 27
Arnold, Benedict 21, 57, 58
Arnold, Obadiah 103, 135
Atcheson, Charles 118

B

Barnes, M.A. 136
Barnes, Sarah 104. *See* Kenan, Sarah
    Barnes
Barrow 63
Bass, H.W. 128
Bayne, Ed 61, 62
Beckham, Mickey 75, 76
Beckham, Samuel 75, 76
Berrien, Judge 140
Berry, George 49
Berry, John 49
Bethune, B.T. 131, 132
Beub, Ed. 128
Big Sam 142
Bill, Dr. Joseph Howland 147, 148
Bird, Thompson 93
Bivins, Shadrack 118
Blount, Reverend Richard M. 139, 140
Bonner, Charles E. 136
Bonner, Jim 113, 114
Bowie, Jim 93
Boykin, Samuel 118
Bradford 27
Brantley, Reverend Edward 98
Breedlove, Mr. 20
Brewer, Matthew 118
Briscoe, Colonel 135

Brooks, Emmett 15, 16
Brown, George A. 118
Brown, Governor Joseph 32
Brown, Mark 118
Bumppo, Natty 26
Burch, Mr. 42
Burgoyne, General John 134
Burnet, Miss 62
Burr, Aaron 22
Bustin, Elenor 117
Byner, Earnest 43
Byrom, Henry 81, 82

C

Calloway 27
Calloway, Dr. 127
Camp 27
Caraker, Jacob 128
Cardonna, Mademoiselle 53
Carnes, Thomas Petters 45
Carr, Arthur 30
Carter, John M. 118
Case, C.L. 127
Case, Dr. 49
Case, Dr. George D. 32
Case, George D. 31, 113
Chatham, Earl of 43, 44
Clark, George 15, 16
Clark, Governor John 19, 41, 42
Clark, John W.R. 19, 20
Clarke, Old Mrs. 145
Cline, P.J. 30
Cline, Peter J. 96
Clinton, Henry 55
Cobb, Ty 27, 28
Collins, David 118
Colquitt, Judge Walter T. 140
Compton 63
Compton, Lyman H. 131
Cone, Judge 140
Cook, Major Phil 121
Cooke, Nicholas 150
Coolidge, President Calvin 86

Cooper, James Fenimore 26
Cornwallis, General Lord Charles 56, 97, 98, 107, 108
Cotting, John Ruggles 13, 14
Covelli, Charles 53
Crawford 135
Crawford, C.P. 128, 131
Crawford, Dr. George 47
Crawford, Mrs. C.P. 85
Crawford, Thomas H. 41, 42
Cresap, Michael 151
Crockett, Davy 52, 93
Cushing, Isaac T. 118
Czar of Russia 130

D

David 27
Dawes, William 133
Decatur, Stephen 137, 138
Denton 63
d'Estaing, Count 55
Duncan, Henry 118
Dunnagan, Senator 142
Dyer, John B. 118

E

Early, Judge Peter 121
Edwards, Warren 128
Elbert, Colonel Samuel 111
Ellis, Thomas M. 81
Ellison 27
Ellison, A.L. 128
Ellison, Oliver 17, 18
Ennis, C.W. 113, 127
Ennis, Elias N. 127, 128, 131
Ennis, P.T. 127, 128
Erwin, U.M. 128
Ethridge, M.W. 136
Eugenie, Mademoiselle 53

F

Fair, Colonel Peter 17
Fair, Judge Peter 103
Fair, Thomas 17, 18
Fannin, James W. 93, 94
Fanny, wife of Old Jim 83
Fenn, W.R. 128

Fields, Senator 142
Flournoy, Polly 87
Flournoy, William 101, 102
Floyd, General John 77
Fogle, Jacob 118
Fort, Dr. Tomlinson 19, 20, 98, 146
Franklin, Benjamin 33
Furman, John H. 136

G

Gardner, Floride 48
Gates, General Horatio 21, 22, 107, 108
Gause, Richard 35
George III, King of England 43
Gerry, Elbridge 149
Gheesling 27
Gibson, C.M. 128
Gibson, James A. 15, 16
Goddard, Fanny 62
Goddard, Joel 128
Goodson, J.W. 128
Greene, General Nathanael 107, 108
Grieve, Miller, Jr. 61, 63
Gwinnett, Button 111, 112

H

Haas, John 52
Hall, Dr. W.H. 131
Hall, Thomas H. 118
Hamilton, Alexander 107
Hamilton, Frank 49
Hammond, Abner 37, 38, 41, 42
Hammond, John 37
Hammond, Sarah 37
Hancock, John 133
Hardeman, Dr. John 113
Harrell 27
Harris, Dr. Iverson L. 113, 131
Harris, George 62
Harris, John 113, 114
Harris, Judge Iverson Louis 103, 139, 140
Harris, William A. 139, 140
Haygood, Charles N. 127, 128, 129, 131
Haygood, Dixie Jarratt 78, 128, 129, 130
Haygood, William 128
Hendrix, H.E. 136
Herty, J.W. 61

Herty, James W. 36
Hewitt, W.C. 135, 136
Hill, David B. 118
Hill, George 87, 88
Hill, Professor D.H., Jr. 113
Hines, Edward R. 95, 96
Holland, Harry 27
Holmes, Ducky 27
Horne, Louise 9
Horne, Mayor 32
Horry, General Peter 33, 34
Horton, Edmond 118
Howard, Gordon 47
Howard, Mary F. 47
Humber, Lula 95, 96
Humber, Mary 95, 96
Humber, R.C. 95
Humphrey, Mrs. 20
Hunt, Benjamin W. 80
Hunter, James 23, 24
Hunter, R.L. 131
Hurst, Lulu 129

I

Ivey, R.D. 136

J

Jackson, President Andrew 52
Jarratt, William D. 118
Jefferson, President Thomas 22
Jemison, Sam 128
Jenkins, Mansfield 136
Jenner, Dr. Edward 19, 20
Joel, Yoel 128
Johnson, John 117, 118
Johnson, Mark 61
Johnson, Thomas 35
Jones, Captain 109
Jones, Jacob 137
Jones, John 136
Jordan, Benjamin S. 25
Jordan, Elizabeth Taylor 25
Jordan, Green Hill 25
Jordan, James K. 32
Jordan, Leonidas 139
Josef, Emperor Franz 130
Joseph, Adolph 61

K

Kenan, Augustus Holmes 101, 103, 104
Kenan, Lewis H. 103, 104
Kenan, Sarah Barnes 104
King, Martin Luther 112
Kirkpatrick, John 118
Kreutz, Henry E. 131, 132

L

Lafayette, General Marquis de 51, 75, 76,
    97
LaFitte, Ed 27
Lamar, Lucius Quintus Cincinnatus 93,
    97, 117, 118, 119
Lamar, Richard 61
Lamar, Sarah Bird 93
Lane, E.P. 36
Lane, Joseph 36
Lane, Mrs. Wm. H. 36
Lanier 27, 28
Launitz, Robert E. 25, 26
Lee, R.E. 61
Lee, Richard Henry 151
Lee, Robert 15, 16
Lincoln, Benjamin 55, 56
Lincoln, President Abraham 55, 56
Little, J.F. 128
Livingston, Janet 57
Locke, Abner 67, 68
Lofton, W.A. 128
Lovejoy, B. 23, 24
Lumpkin, Judge Joseph 140
Lumpkin, William 19
Lyman, Daniel 49

M

Madison, President James 22
Mapp, F.B. 131
Mapp, Frank 30
Marion, Francis 33, 34
Marlor, John 142
Mathews, Charles 137, 138
McAdoo, William Gibbs 85, 86
McComb, Robert 81, 82
McCombs, Robert 118
McCrary, Bartley 118
McElvoy, Representative 142

McIntosh, General Lachlan 111, 112
McIntosh, George 111
McKinley, Cadet Captain William 32
McKinley, President William 32
McMillan, Tom 27
Mitchell, David Brydie 34
Montgomery, Field Marshal Bernard Law 57
Montgomery, General Richard 57, 58
Moore, Mrs. Charles 85
Moore, Mrs. R.B. 85
Morgan, Daniel 151
Myrick, Sallie 135, 136
Myrick, Stith P. 135, 136

N

Nailor, Mr. 49
Napier 63
Nosworthy, J.M. 136
Nunnally 27

O

O'Daniel, Dr. 30
Old Jim 83
Orme 63
Orme, Richard M. 118
Otis, James 133

P

Palmer, Miss 121, 122
Pasteur, Dr. Louis 80
Peale, Charles Willson 67
Pemberton, A.H. 142
Pemberton, Francis 118
Perry, H. 136
Pickett, Richard 118
Pitt, William 43, 44
Plattney, Hiram 109
Powell, Dr. 30, 127
Powell, Dr. T.O. 131
Prosser, John 118
Prosser, Thomas 136
Putnam, General Israel 133

R

Ramsey, Judge 128
Ray, William D. 118

Reddy, Isham 118
Reese, General Augustus 140
Reese, Seaborn 128
Reid, S.A. 47
Revere, Paul 133, 134
Riddle, A.J. 63
Robbins, Anna H. 135, 136
Roberts, R.W. 140
Robertson, Felix 145
Robertson, James 145, 146
Robinson, Solomon 118
Roosevelt, President Theodore 15, 16
Rucker, Nap 27

S

Sallie 63
Sanford, F.H. 140
Sanford, General John W.A. 139
Sanford, Hershel V. 61
Sanford, Judge D.B. 113, 128
Sanford, Richard H. 139, 140
Sanford, Sol 15, 16
Schley, Governor William 94
Schuyler, General Philip 57
Scogin, John 128
Scott, George W. 15, 16
Scott, John B. 77
Scott, W.H. 131
Shafter, General William R. 31
Simmons, Dr. Benjamin Judson 99, 100
Sims, Dr. 127
Skinner, Jacob 67
Slater, Clementine 99
Smith, Alfred E. 85, 86
Smith, Dr. 127
Smith, Lemuel 101
Smith, Levin J. 118
Smith, Solomon 101, 102, 142
Smith, Thomas 128
Snead, John T. 135, 136
Spalding, James 137, 138
Spalding, Sarah 138
Spalding, Thomas 137, 138
Speights, Levi 118
Staley, Joseph 131
Stapleton, Senator 142
Strother, John R. 103, 104

Stubbs, Baradel P. 118
Supple, James 128
Swann 27

T

Talbert, Benjamin 97, 98
Talbert, Joseph 97
Talbert, Rebeccah 97
Talmadge, Reverend Samuel K. 35
Tarleton, Colonel Banastre 97
Taylor 27
Thacher, Dr. James 151
Thomas, E.H. 128
Thomas, Eliza 59
Thomas, James 83
Thomas, Jett 59, 77, 78
Thomas, John Sherrod 59, 60
Thomas, Martha 83
Torrence, W.H. 136
Troutman, Hiram 93
Troutman, Joanna 93, 94
Troutman, John 93
Trumbull, Jonathan 150
Tucker, Adele Louise 143, 144
Tucker, W.J. 128
Tucker, William Henry 143
Turner, Jacob P. 118

V

Vance, Dr. Patrick 145, 146
Villa, Pancho 15
Vinson, Carl 95, 96

W

Wales, Prince of 130
Walls, E.H. 136
Ward, Colonel 81, 82
Warren, General Joseph 133, 134
Warrington, Lewis 137
Washington, General George 21, 22, 33,
        55, 56, 98, 107, 108, 112, 117, 134,
        149, 150, 151, 152, 153
Wayne, General Anthony 22, 105, 106
Wayne, Isaac 105, 106
Wayne, Margarita 105
Weems, John B. 135
Weems, Mason Locke 33, 34

West, Joseph 118
West, Thomas 61, 62
Whaley, Mary 97
Wheeler, General Joe 31
Whiddon 63
Whilden, G.T. 131
Whitaker, Dr. 30
Whitaker, Dr. J.C. 62
Whitaker, Dr. J.M. 127
Whitaker, J.M. 61
Whitaker, Maggie 62
Whitaker, Simon 41, 42
White, Dr. Benjamin Aspinwall 60
White, Dr. Samuel G. 69
White, Professor H.C. 113, 114
Whitfield, Solicitor General 128
Wilhelm, Kaiser 130
Wilkinson 27
Wilkinson, Dawson 128
Wilkinson, James 21, 22
Williams, Peter J. 142
Williamson, W. 61
Wilson 63
Wilson, Carlos G. 128
Wilson, Dr. Robert 21, 22
Wilson, Eleanor 85
Wilson, President Woodrow 85
Windsor, T.T. 131
Wright, Pryor 118
Wright Brothers 109
Wynne, A.F. 128

Y

Young, James 118
Young, Representative 142

Z

Zachry, James 87

Visit us at
www.historypress.net